THE WRONG KIND OF JEW

A MIZRAHI MANIFESTO

BY HEN MAZZIG

WICKED SON

WICKED SON   Post Hill PRESS

Post Hill Press
New York • Nashville
WickedSonBooks.com

Published in the United States of America

1 2 3 4 5 6 7 8 9 10

CONTENTS

INTRODUCTION

One of the first things people learn about me is that I'm Jewish.

When people ask me what I do for a living, "I'm Jewish" is usually the shorthand answer. For the past ten years, I have worked as a "professional Jew" touring the world to educate audiences about the Jewish story—our past, our present, and our hopeful future.

At this point, I don't know what facet of my life isn't entrenched in Judaism, who in my life knows me outside of it, or where I've gone without a Star of David (both metaphorically and physically) hanging around my neck.

When people ask what I'm passionate about, Judaism, likely, comes first. If you ask where I'm from, the answer is Israel, so usually a dead giveaway. But if you dive into my ethnicity or race, I will tell you that my family comes from North Africa and the Middle East—Tunisia, and Iraq, to be more specific.

"So you're Arab?" people often ask. And I respond, "No, *I'm a Jew."*

I'm Mizrahi. The Jews of the Middle East and North Africa are known as Mizrahim. But few people—Jewish and non-Jewish alike—know of us. There are many reasons for that, one of which is that for too many, Mizrahim are "the wrong kind of Jew." We're not only unfamiliar, our culture shatters stereotypes and unspoken rules. Meanwhile, our story derails the narrative many want to propagate about Jews, antisemitism, and most controversially, Israel. We break the expectations many hold about Jews and race, the Middle East and religion, and even politics and oppression.

I've been "the wrong kind of Jew" my entire life, and not just because of my ethnic background.

I don't eat Kosher. My partner is non-Jewish. I rarely go to temple on Friday nights. In fact, I pick up my phone and tweet on Shabbat, the weekly twenty-four-hour period Jews are obligated to rest—honestly, I don't think I've taken a day of rest in years.

I don't abide by most Jewish laws. Especially whichever one said being gay isn't allowed. I break that rule on pretty much a daily basis. (As does the man I've asked to marry me.)

So there's that.

But because of Mizrahi heritage, I don't fit into what many people see as the secular, cultural tenets of Judaism. For example, I like bagels, but I don't consider them *my* cuisine. I don't have opinions on Katz Deli or whether or not they are better than Langer's. What kind of meat is pastrami?

I'm still not sure. My Saturday lunch can be okra, pink beets, pumpkin or hard-boiled eggs with Hummus, and a pita bread. My grandma doesn't make matzo-ball soup when I'm sick, or even on the holidays. Instead, she's making stew that most of my Jewish friends can't pronounce.

My grandparents don't look or sound like Larry David, Sarah Silverman or Bernie Sanders. Actually, they more closely resemble the Arabs who owned the chicken restaurant Larry called "an antisemitic shithole" on an episode of *Curb Your Enthusiasm*. Or the tan cartoon Pharaoh in *Prince of Egypt* shouting, "I will hear no more of this Hebrew nonsense!"

Speaking of which, my surname isn't very Hebrew sounding. Somehow it always gets me an extra pat-down in airport security—even in my home country of Israel. No matter how expensive my shirt is, my beard still gets me a few suspicious glances on the airplane. Or perhaps it's my accent.

Yes, my grandparents were in the Holocaust. Can't get more Jewish than that, right? But their streets were never lined with swastikas or German soldiers. No one scrawled "*Jude*" on their homes or businesses. My grandma and grandpa didn't survive Auschwitz or Dachau or Buchenwald. They were due to be sent to Nazi camps whose names are unknown. Their neighbors were shot and raped in antisemitic riots which most people, even most synagogues, don't commemorate.

It's not that I don't fit a Jewish stereotype—I just don't relate to the culture that most people in the West define as *Jewish*. Because it isn't mine.

I don't nestle neatly to the expectations we have about Jewish people. I experience prejudice because I'm Jewish, but unfortunately, from both Jews and non-Jews. I've had my life threatened by neo-Nazis, but many fellow Jews have taken issue with me on the basis of my race and sexuality. Because of how I look or whom I love, some do not perceive me as Jewish at all. To them, at best, I am not "really Jewish," which is their way of saying "the wrong kind of Jewish."

And sometimes I get it. I'm bad at calling out antisemitism when it's politically useful. I can't help but speak out when I see hatred from people, regardless of which ideological team they play for. When the right is happy with me, I call out bigotry among their ranks.

When I finally have proven I am liberal enough, I put a spotlight on how progressive movements exclude Jews. I have the audacity to be an Israeli who does not believe that Israel is the perfect utopia they told you about in Hebrew school. But I understand that things don't have to be perfect to be beautiful. Beautiful enough to risk your life and reputation for.

Speaking of reputations, I'm not afraid to call out when your role model or celebrity crush expresses hatred against Jews. But when many want to steamroll someone for their ignorance regarding Judaism, I'm often that fellow trying to educate rather than punish the perpetrator. I try to find redemption for people half the town wants to burn at the stake.

I'm bad at meeting the appropriate narrative. I can't tell my story of beating back hatred against Jews, about the millennia of subservience my ancestors survived, without mentioning that Mizrahi Jews still face inequalities today.

I'm not the kind of Jew who keeps our dirty laundry off the clothesline.

But I'm certainly not the kind of Jew who wants to hang our people out to dry.

I'm not a silent Jew, not a blanket to give cover to antisemites. Bigots cannot buy my silence, even at the price of acceptance. I'm not the Jew who chooses politics over truth, who will protect my friends over my people. I will not kneel before any movement when they refuse to offer Jews a seat at the table.

No matter how polite they appear, I refuse to appease bigots, even when they offer me solidarity. When I feel rejected by the Jewish society, I don't scour for acceptance from their adversaries. I am not their "good Jew." For I know there are no good Jews to antisemites. There is nothing good about being Jewish to them. However, a Jew pushing hateful ideology against our own people is useful. And I ask: why be useful when you can be bad?

I am the wrong kind of Jew for so many, a bad Jew. I'm bad at meeting expectations of what Jewish looks like, sounds like, thinks like, and means. I'm bad at looking the other way when bigotry comes from within our community *and* from people who claim to stand up for marginalized groups but hold hatred, ignorance, and apathy toward Jews.

I'm also "divisive." I can't help but say that Jews like me exist, our experiences are different from the mainstream, and we deserve respect and humanity. I keep bringing up my family's history, even when there's no room for it in the textbook.

Worst of all, I keep being Jewish—and loudly so. No matter how I fail to live up to so many people's ideals, I never stop owning my Jewish heritage. I refuse to be quiet about it. My Star of David lives around my neck and is never tucked underneath my t-shirt.

I have the audacity to know that I am a bad Jew and feel good about it. To love every minute of being Jewish on this earth, and the legacy of every Jew before me—including but not limited to Mizrahim.

Because deep down, I know the contradictions that have labeled me a so-called "wrong kind of Jew" are aligned with the tenants and traditions of Judaism.

I ask questions. Not benign, polite questions. I have complicated ones. When I get a query myself, I give even harder answers.

l do not assimilate. l do not give up my own essence with all my complexities, even if it will appease those who wish my downfall.

l believe in history. Do you know that it takes the sun's light eight and one-third minutes to reach us on earth? So, while we are living in this moment, everything around us is elucidated by the past. There are countless rays of light behind us, and by telling the full story of the Jewish people— and the world as a whole—we can all see a little better.

It's time that the story of Mizrahi Jews finally is told, to the Jewish community and world at large. This story cannot just be about our past, our cuisine, or culture. It has to go deeper, discussing the real contradictions we stand in, the invisibility that taints our experience, and actionable ways we can achieve full equality and dignity. l am not the only man who can write the Mizrahi story, but l am the only one who can tell *my* Mizrahi story. My tale crosses countries, conti- nents, boundaries, and controversies. Mizrahim don't need a history book. We don't need a memoir. We need a manifesto, and damn it, mine is personal, for nothing is more intimate than one's ancestry and identity.

l am not going to present the Mizrahi experience like a textbook or an assortment of artifacts under plexiglass at a museum. We are going to take the Mizrahi story out of its frame, touch it, even leave a few fingerprints. l don't want you to just read about being Mizrahi, but to experience it too. To really understand history, you have to feel it as well. That's how I can see my whole self—and you.

I see you.

I see you, and if you are Jewish, I ask: are you my kind of Jew?

Which ideals do you fail to live up to? Which contradictions do you hold? Who are you by being yourself, letting down? Who are you saving? What uncomfortable conversations are you starting? Whose ignorance are you unraveling?

There's nothing more Jewish than refusing the world's expectations of who you are and ignoring their judgment. Maybe if we all decide to be the *wrong* kind of Jews together, we can be Jewish the *right* way.

1.

HATING HEN

"Hide behind the wall until it's safe," a student urgently whispers to me. She is visibly shaking, yet somehow composed enough to tell me what to do.

The baroque clocks of University College London have just struck seven. A security guard informs us that we—myself and the two dozen students who have come to hear me speak—are being redirected to another classroom. It's our third venue of the evening as the enraged crowd outside has, once again, discovered our location.

A cell phone rings, belonging to a security guard. After an inaudible call, he rushes me into the classroom.

Though the protesters have yet to spot me, I can still hear their chants ring out:

"Where is Hen?"

"No murderers on our campus!"

"Shame! Shame! Shame!"

More than a dozen students await my arrival in the class-room, their bodies trembling with fear. What was intended to be an innocent campus event now feels more like a hostage situation.

"Stay inside," Liora orders. She's the student who orga-nized the event and invited me to speak at UCL. If the protest-ers (a generous description, I might add) see us this time, we will assuredly be surrounded and, consequently, under siege. Years of experience in the military dealing with hostile situa-tions never prepared me for this evening.

Moments later, the police start to shout: "Everyone, get inside! Fast!" The mob has discovered our location.

I see at least five students sprint toward us, attempting to shove their way into the room while guards struggle to pin the doors shut. The aggressors are unsuccessful but continue to slam their fists against the classroom windows to show that they won't be backing down easily.

I hear the pounding of drums, peppered with repeated chants calling for the death of Israel. They quickly line up outside the windows, rattling the shutters and thumping their hands against the glass. My own name becomes part of a chilling mantra: "Hen, war criminal!"

This happened in 2016. I had been invited to speak at a cam-pus cultural event coordinated by British Jewish students.

England was my last stop on an international speaking tour, and while my trip to North America had been a huge success, London proved to be more of a challenge.

This wasn't my first run-in with students in Britain, either. Two years earlier, I had been invited to speak at King's College London by the pro-Israel student group there. It was my first foray into what would turn out to be years of being protested by hundreds of students on campuses around the world.

The students protesting that night back in 2014 at King's College had a particular demand of their school administration: prevent my "criminal" feet from ever touching campus grounds. In their eyes, to allow me, Hen Mazzig, to speak at their school was analogous to abetting a murderer.

Though the administrators at King's didn't cave to the demands of those students, my speech was greeted with a childish, yet intimidating, stunt by one of the anti-Israel groups on campus. Despite my politely inviting them to stay and listen to my talk in the interest of having a respectful dialogue, they exited the room with taped mouths while holding signs scribbled with hateful messages. including calls for the death of Israel.

As it turned out, likely because they didn't make any attempts to respectfully engage, their protest was misguided and unfounded. They weren't protesting anything I had actually done or even said; rather, they objected to the very notion that my country had a right to exist.

Admittedly, the experience at King's was more disturbing than terrifying. So I thought I knew what to expect when I arrived at UCL two years later.

Weeks before the event was to take place, the Jewish student group that had invited me began to face extreme pressure from anti-Israel activists to rescind its offer. Just days prior to my arrival, Students' Union UCL, the representative body for University College London, actually tried to cancel the event after students sent threatening letters to the group sponsoring it. Again, the university's administration thankfully ruled in favor of free speech, so my talk could go ahead. However, the public calls to shut us down didn't stop.

The moment my plane landed on British soil, I received a barrage of messages informing me that anti-Israel activists, students, and others were spreading hysteria about me and the event on social media. One particular London-based extremist group called Friends of Al-Aqsa incited a violent mob. They called me a murderer, a war criminal, and accused me of directly participating in massacres of Palestinians.

It is probably worth mentioning at this point that I have never killed anyone. While I did serve in the Israel Defense Forces COGAT (Coordinator of Government Activities in the Territories) unit, which is in charge of civil communication and security coordination with the Palestinian Authority, our unit's sole purpose was to preserve peace and keep both Israeli and Palestinian civilians safe and secure. My military service was focused on the practice of de-escalation and enhancing quality of life for Palestinian civilians. It was both administrative and humanitarian in nature.

But when a mob is enraged at you for perceived wrong-doings, no facts matter. Nothing I have ever done or fought for—including things many members of this mob, in a more sober moment, would probably agree with—are of any consequence.

It's now seven thirty in the evening, and I am crammed inside the classroom with an audience of roughly twenty-five devoted Jewish students as well as a few members of the Jewish community who are here to show support.

As I get ready to speak, loud calls of "Intifada! Intifada!" echo through the halls and into the room. As the speaker, I want to present a strong, even nonchalant façade. But inside, I am suffocating from the hate. I am suddenly pulled back to when I was twelve years old, when I was nearly killed in a suicide bombing during the second intifada. Traumatic images start flashing through my mind.

Amid the pounding and chants, a window facing out toward the campus shatters. Four protesters leap through the opening and into the room. Reliving my own trauma, I turn to see Jewish students on the ground crying and pleading. I can see terror in their eyes.

For these protesters, it isn't enough simply to express their disapproval of my presence, a right granted to individuals in most Western nations. To them, my talk is so dangerous that I have to be silenced with violence.

Security tells the invaders to leave, but they refuse. They have officially claimed this space. I find myself hugging a female student who is having a panic attack, her ragged breaths causing me more frustration than fear.

Part of me wants physically to fight back. But I don't want to sink to their level. I know many of the students here to deplatform me are deliberately trying to provoke a reaction, and I am also keenly aware of how the media would frame any sort of retaliation. In all likelihood, I would be blamed.

This is because the media have a nasty habit of blaming Jews for fighting back, insinuating that a Jew must have provoked the antisemitism against himself.

This pattern would be repeated three months later when UCL issued a biased report of the incident without even seeking my account. Severely inaccurate from top to bottom, the report attempted to frame those seeking to silence me as *victims*, mentioning the term *Islamophobia* more than eighty times while addressing antisemitism just once. Somewhat absurdly, the mob's calls for a violent intifada were described as a "legitimate and legal protest."

I decide to not fight back, so I do my best to let go of my rage and instead focus on calming the room. Maintaining restraint, and therefore our dignity, amid the tumult is paramount to our safety and well-being.

It is fortunate that when we relocated to this classroom, students inside were able to barricade the doors before the protesters found us. The protesters who had shattered the windows minutes earlier eventually leave of their own volition and rejoin the mob outside.

Finally, forty-five minutes after the scheduled start time, I begin to speak. At the sound of my voice, the activists outside grow furious, roaring even louder than before. "Intifada! Intifada! Intifada!"

A sound system has been set up outside, its speakers aimed directly at the classroom. Bass notes of Arabic rap music send vibrations through the room. Until this moment, I'd never known it was possible to weaponize music.

At this point, a team of campus security staff, also outside, is just watching, impotent.

I'm determined to carry on, so I eagerly launch into the story of my Mizrahi heritage and that of hundreds of thousands of Jews who were ethnically cleansed from the Arab Middle East. I speak about how the evening's assault—both verbal and physical—brings to mind the Farhud, a violent spree of murder, rape, and dispossession against Iraqi Jews, including my mother's family, in 1941. Those were days of massacres that my Iraqi Jewish grandmother, somehow, survived.

I cannot allow the mob to silence my family's story. So I continue, beaten down internally though undeterred externally. Making a show of strength, both for myself and those in attendance, is key to getting through this night. So I speak about my service in COGAT, how I survived a terror attack as a child, and my work with the LGBTQ community in Israel.

Though I struggle to talk over the noise of the protest, it is at this moment, after the hundreds of talks I've given across the world, that I actually pour out my soul for the first time. "It is this violence that my grandparents faced in Iraq, and that the Jews have endured throughout the centuries. I'm in so much pain to see you facing this today, but I promise I will never stop fighting for you," I tell the shaken students.

I finish my speech and reassure the crowd that I would gladly return, and that neither I nor they will be silenced. This, I tell them, is what Zionism has always been about. "We won tonight," I affirm as we all stand up and sing "Hatikvah" ("The Hope"), Israel's national anthem.

We sing louder than the noise surrounding us, just like the last Jews of Masada did while committing to their Jewish heritage as the Romans completed their vanquishing of the Jewish communities of Judea, including the destruction of Jerusalem, in the first century CE. In this instant, even in the face of brutality and harassment, our music gives us a sense of transcendent safety and even pride.

The feelings of comfort are fleeting, however.

As I leave, I am hurried off campus, hidden by the coat of one of the twenty police officers who have arrived late, just in time for the event to end. They repeat their orders, "Don't look back, keep running," until I finally emerge onto the streets of London. The protesters get in one last verbal lick before I can fully escape. "Go home!" someone shouts at me.

The irony in this taunt, of course, is that the very people who want me to "go home" also don't want me to have a home at all. Herein lies the disturbing paradox of the modern-day anti-Israel, anti-Zionist movement.

UCL was not an isolated incident. Wherever I speak about my experiences and views, I seem to trigger a visceral, irrational anger among a certain group of people. I draw their rage like a moth to an irresistible flame.

Frequently, these attacks come from people who, according to conventional wisdom, one might expect to support me the most: intellectuals, journalists, and social justice activists. So it was in 2019 when I wrote an op-ed in the *Los Angeles Times* entitled, "No, Israel isn't a country of privileged and powerful white Europeans."

In the article, I debunked a myth that has taken hold in certain circles: Israel is a majority-White country that is hell-bent on oppressing people of color. Quite the contrary, I said, the majority of Israel's population are actually Mizrahi Jews who, like myself, are people of color. We serve in the Israeli military and in the government. The myth, I pointed out, is part of an ideology that frames Israel as a colonialist aggressor while wholly ignoring not only its actual demographic make-up but also its history as a safe haven for those fleeing oppression.

One person who apparently didn't like what I wrote was Marc Lamont Hill. An esteemed professor at Temple University, Hill lost his job as a CNN commentator in 2018 after using the popular Palestinian chant "from the [Jordan] river to the [Mediterranean] sea"[1] (which many view as a call for Israel's destruction) during a meeting at the United Nations. Hill put me on blast before his ninety thousand Facebook followers, claiming that I ignored "the racial and political project that transformed Palestinian Jews (who lived peacefully with other Palestinians) into the twentieth-century identity category of 'Mizrahi' as a means of detaching them from Palestinian identity.... Israel can be racially diverse and still be a site of white supremacy."[2]

Hill, a self-styled expert on the Israeli-Palestinian conflict, was accusing me of invoking a fabricated "identity category." In other words, I'm not really Mizrahi, because Mizrahi is not really a thing. I merely *think* I'm the proud son of Tunisian and Iraqi Jews who had a unique history and identity and zero historical connection to Palestinian Arabs. In fact, according to Hill, what I really am is a Palestinian Arab who is being used as a tool of white supremacy.

Imagine for a moment if I told people that I studied race relations and the civil rights movement in the United States, and then made claims about how the African American "identity category" was invented as part of a White supremacist project. Hill, I suspect, would be rightly outraged. Yet he—a man who doesn't speak our language, hasn't lived in our homeland, and doesn't understand our culture—was doing exactly this.

Never mind that the vast majority of Mizrahi Israelis were not from Palestine, but rather from Morocco, Iraq, and other Arab countries. Never mind the fact that Jews living in Palestine before the emergence of Zionism never called the land "Palestine" (they used the ancient Hebrew term *Eretz Yisrael*, the Land of Israel) or had any kind of shared Palestinian identity with the local Arab population.

As Mizrahis in Israel know, our identity emerged both as a result of a shared experience we had over centuries across the Muslim world before being expelled, as well as a challenge to the Ashkenazi Jews who called the shots in Israel in its first three decades. (Of course, Ashkenazi Jews themselves came to Palestine to escape the European racism that had treated them as subhumans for centuries.)

Another notable activist who joined the campaign against me was Linda Sarsour, former co-chair of the Women's March.

Sarsour, who outrageously asserted in a 2017 interview with *The Nation* that one couldn't be both a Zionist and a feminist, piled onto Hill's post, commenting that I stay relevant by mentioning hers and Hill's names in my writing. Apparently, if I voice criticism of people trying to erase me, that's just me trying to "stay relevant."

This wasn't the first time Sarsour had targeted me. A few years earlier, she took to Twitter to chastise me for celebrating Pride Month, even though I am a proud Israeli gay man. "Selective memory," she tweeted at me in response. "Remember the stabbing at the pride parade in Israel?"[3] She was referring to a tragic incident during the 2015 Jerusalem pride parade when an ultra-Orthodox extremist stabbed sixteen-year-old Shira Banki to death. But as horrible as it was, why should a crime against gays disqualify me from celebrating our pride? According to Sarsour, the answer would likely be because it happened in Israel, where it seems like none of the rules of good-faith judgment apply.

Sarsour, of course, loves to speak on behalf of communities about which she has very little knowledge. She was born and raised in New York City, where she lives today, and she is not a part of the LGBTQ community. As such, a pride parade in Jerusalem has virtually no impact on her life.

Sarsour took yet another swing at me a year later. Commenting on a tweet of mine challenging her on the issue of antisemitism, she accused me of racism by saying, "Says

the guy who harasses Black Jewish voices on Twitter. Stop it."[4]
She went radio silent, however, when Black Jewish rapper
Westside Gravy responded: "Linda, who are you to speak for
Black Jews? We have voices and are capable of using them.
Stop using us to attack leaders like Hen Mazzig who uplift
voices that don't fit your narrative, and have defended Black
Jews like myself on multiple occasions."[5]

Several months later, I was in the process of planning an
American speaking tour. A handful of Jewish leaders in states
like Ohio and Florida protested my appearances, events
which were scheduled by members of their own community.
Detractors claimed I was a "Right-wing Twitter troll" who
attacks Muslim women like Sarsour and Black men like Marc
Lamont Hill on social media. Although I had never targeted
anyone due to their race or religion—treatment I would never
want to be done to me—this intimidation campaign led to a
few of my events getting canceled.

While I was trying to counter Hill's and Sarsour's attempts
to erase my identity and gaslight my people, a deeper question troubled me. Why would public figures like them, woke
celebs with hundreds of thousands of followers who casually
ignore the vast majority of their critics, go out of their way to
attack *me*?

I had to be striking a nerve.

Perhaps more predictably, the nerve I was hitting wasn't
just with people on the Left. Over the years, I have also been

targeted by White supremacists who repeatedly used images of my face to create fake antisemitic accounts and share incendiary memes on social media. They have even, on several occasions, publicly shared my home address, solely as an intimidation tactic.

Attacks from Right-wing groups didn't end with social media trolling. Leaders of pro-Israel organizations like the Zionist Organization of America have accused me of siding with terrorists over my fellow Israeli soldiers when I've expressed support for peace with Palestine. David Ha'ivri, a settler leader from the Samaria Regional Council, called me "disingenuous and obnoxious" and asserted that I "repeat a lot of the things that [anti-Israel activists] are saying about Israel...with the same goal as BDS."[6] The Boycott, Divestment and Sanctions movement (BDS) is a Palestinian-led movement promoting boycotts, divestments, and economic sanctions against Israel.

I have received more tweets from politically conservative Jews accusing me of dividing the Jewish community or of hating Ashkenazi Jews than I even care to count at this point. Not to mention the constant drumbeat of hate I get from Right-wingers disgusted by pictures on social media of my partner and me enjoying our lives together—that's just the icing of bigotry on the multilayered harassment cake.

Something about me—my unusual combination of being outspoken, Zionist, gay, and non-White—just seems to get under people's skin. Sure, I am a relatively staunch defender of Israel, and sometimes it might seem like I'm looking for a fight. But many people who speak openly about supporting Israel don't get this kind of white-hot vitriol.

What makes me different?

For years, I just carried on. I'm not the type to back down, especially when my country and my identity are under attack. While fighting back has admittedly grown my following and resulted in more speaking invitations, it's also led to a ratcheting up of the assault against me.

It took a long time, but over the years I slowly began to realize what, in fact, made me different. It wasn't that I am gay, or progressive, or even that I am a Zionist who served in the IDF (Israel Defense Forces). Really, it was just one specific aspect of my identity, above all the others, that was driving people up a wall.

It was that I'm Mizrahi.

For example, it's the only explanation for the assault I endured from American scholars of Jewish and Israel studies—a discipline where you'd expect sympathy for a gay peace activist raising the profile of his non-European heritage.

In December 2019, an article appeared on George Washington University's History News Network called, "How did November become the Mizrahi Heritage Month? And what's Mizrahi anyhow?" Co-authored by the chair of Israel studies at George Washington University, Arie M. Dubnov, and Lior Sternfeld[7] of the Jewish studies department at Penn State University, the piece presented an argument specifically targeting me and my Mizrahi identity.

Although the article was couched in soft, academic, on-the-other-hand language, the crux of its claim was that proud assertions of modern-day Mizrahi identity, represented by people like me and groups like JIMENA that promote Mizrahi Heritage Month, are actually a secret plot by the Israeli government to further an agenda deeply rooted in propaganda. JIMENA (Jews Indigenous to the Middle East and North Africa), a nonprofit organization headquartered in the San Francisco Bay Area, works to preserve Mizrahi and Sephardic culture and history through educating the public and advocating for Jewish refugees from the Middle East. Dubnov and Sternfeld, who are Ashkenazi, took pains to dismiss JIMENA as "right-leaning" and "quick to adopt the Israeli ready-made mold of 'Mizrahi commemoration,'" before turning their focus on me personally:

> Similar ideas are expressed by Hen Mazzig, a charismatic yet controversial "Hasbarah" (pro-Israeli advocacy) speaker.... It remains unclear if these are grassroots initiatives or a well-orchestrated state-funded campaign. As the Jewish daily *The Forward* revealed, Mazzig is most probably a contractor paid by the Israeli government....

They went on to say, albeit not about me directly:

We raise our eyebrows, however, at what seems as what might be an attempt to hijack this noble cause for a partisan issue and a state-sponsored invented tradition.

Reading this article left me no less dumbfounded than disgusted. The claim that I am a secret Israeli agent was originally based on a poorly researched article by a lazy junior reporter at the *Forward*, who inflated the fact that I had, years earlier, consulted for a government civil service body, work that was unrelated to my career as a human rights advocate. Notwithstanding the academic bona fides of Dubnov and Sternfeld, their article was nothing more than a conspiracy theory attacking both the Mizrahi identity and my own credibility.

While neither Dubnov nor Sternfeld are Mizrahi, they do represent a large majority of the Jewish studies establishment, especially in the United States. They view Mizrahi and Sephardi Jews as a tiny and mostly irrelevant stream within Orthodoxy that holds little influence against the ocean of Yiddish-language and European Jewish history.

Fortunately, other scholars show greater understanding of our identity. In his meticulous, award-winning book *The End of Judaism in Muslim Lands*, historian Shmuel Trigano of Paris Nanterre University presents a powerful rebuttal to Sternfeld and Dubnov.

As Trigano explains, the best way to understand Mizrahim is by unifying the narratives of Jews who were expelled from different Middle Eastern and North African countries during the twentieth century. The exodus of our people, he argues, constituted a common history. Our shared cultural, political, and linguistic heritage, alongside our collective experience in the face of unified action against us by the Arab League, are central to who we are as a people:

> The Jews of the Arab countries suffered from per-secution and pogroms for many generations, hundreds of years prior to the emergence of Zionism.... Their situation deteriorated in modern times and the appearance of Arab nationalism in the 20th century. The narrative that describes their immigration to Israel as colonialism is the opposite of the truth. These were fleeing refugees who found home and shelter in the State of Israel.[8]

As the son of an Iraqi Jewish mother and Tunisian Jewish father, I find the link between the two sides of my family's experience indisputable. It is also documented history, unlike the defensive speculations of American scholar-activists like Dubnov and Sternfeld.

What's more bizarre is the wildly erroneous claim that the Mizrahi identity is a "well-orchestrated state-funded campaign" of the Israeli government. As I will discuss later, for decades after the founding of Israel, the Ashkenazi-dominated political elites of the country did everything they could to *suppress* both Mizrahi and European identities in favor of a new form of "Israeliness." Even if it were true that today the government supports efforts to promote Mizrahi identity around the world—and it may very well be, for all I know—it's only because Mizrahim in the country found their own voice and expressed it at the ballot box. Israel is a representative democracy where at least half of all voters are Mizrahi, and Mizrahim constitute the central voting base for parties on the Right, which have held power for most of the last four decades. So even if the Israeli government in the last generation represents the interests of Mizrahim in the way critics describe, would it really be so bad if a modicum of funding went toward affirming our heritage?

The claims coming from Jewish American scholars or from Marc Lamont Hill, however, are borne not out of familiarity with Israel, but out of their own political imperative. This mentality includes a hatred of the Israeli Right so deep that they will paint self-assertive Mizrahim as part of a government conspiracy.

Faced with the uncomfortable reality that non-White, non-European Mizrahim have become a powerful force in defining Israeli, and therefore Jewish, history, some people prefer just to erase our identity altogether.

It happens that I don't support the Israeli Right and have never voted for Likud, their political party. My criticisms of former prime minister Benjamin Netanyahu's policies, both diplomatic and social, are sharp, and I voice them often on Twitter and in my editorial writing. The truth is that attempts by Sternfeld and Dubnov, or Sarsour and Hill, or anybody else, to depict me—a champion of Palestinian self-determination, Black Lives Matter, and gender and LGBTQ equality—as a Right-wing shill says a lot more about them than it does about me.

What exactly is Mizrahi?

The majority of Jews in France are Mizrahim. So are many Jews in Canada and South America, as well as scattered populations across the Middle East and Central Asia, from Morocco to Azerbaijan. But the biggest community of Mizrahim is in Israel. We are, in fact, a majority of the country's Jews—between three and four million of us—and our unique culture and history have a significant impact on what it means to be Israeli, who our leaders are, and how the country's culture looks.

You cannot understand Israel *at all*, or what being Jewish means in the twenty-first century, if you don't understand Mizrahim.

If you're an educated Jew who grew up in America, you probably heard about Sephardic Jews. They are the descendants of Jews who were expelled from Spain and Portugal in the fifteenth century and developed their own synagogues and customs. Since many of them ended up in the Middle East, where they joined older Jewish communities dating back to biblical times, and because Americans seem to struggle with too many identity categories, "Sephardic" has become a stand-in term for every Jew who isn't Ashkenazi—that is, those whose ancestry isn't traced to Central and Eastern Europe. They are the strange Jews whose families never spoke Yiddish, never ate gefilte fish or knishes, and who, for the most part, didn't endure the horrors of the Holocaust. And because more than 90 percent of American Jews are Ashkenazi, many don't give the category much thought.

If you're Jewish, you probably grew up believing that the choices for Jewish identity were mainly denominational—Orthodox, Conservative, Reform, Reconstructionist, or "just Jewish." You probably were taught that Jewish identity was mainly about what kind of synagogue you attended, what type of food you ate, or what causes you supported. I mean, can one be authentically Jewish without absorbing some Yiddish words, watching *Seinfeld*, and eating bagels?

All along, as you were preparing for your Bar or Bat Mitzvah and going to temple for the High Holy Days, you may not even have been aware that there's an entirely alternative Jewish culture that's been around for centuries and is the defining identity for millions of Jews. It's a fascinating history of rich traditions without the same hang-ups, music, and humor as the Judaism you know. It's different, and it's beautiful.

Today, Mizrahim are the dominant cultural force in Israel. This is a giant leap forward from the middle of the last century when we were expelled from countries like Morocco, Tunisia, Libya, Syria, Iraq, Iran, Yemen, and others—places where we'd lived for centuries. We didn't speak Yiddish (a mix of Hebrew and German) or any of the other local languages Jews spoke in Eastern Europe. Instead, we had our own Jewish languages that blended Hebrew with elements of Arabic, Persian, and Spanish. And just like the Jews of Eastern Europe, we too developed our own Jewish food and music.

When we broke away from Orthodox practice, it wasn't a clean break. We didn't do Reform, the way the Jews of Germany did before they brought it to the United States, or Conservative, the way American Jews did in response to new trends in academic scholarship. Instead, we established a fluid kind of traditionalism. In Israel, we developed our own politics and an entire genre of music that's become more popular than Israeli Western-style pop. If you're wondering why Israeli Jews are so different from American Jews, a big part of it is because the country has been heavily influenced by Mizrahim.

And contrary to common belief, many of us experienced the Holocaust. During World War II, Morocco, Algeria, and Tunisia were ruled by the Nazis, either directly or through the Vichy government, and many of us were sent to death camps. My Tunisian grandparents worked at a forced labor camp and would have been sent off for extermination if the war hadn't ended just days before the transport was supposed to leave.

But even in places where the swastika never flew, we were victims of the war. The Farhud, the 1941 pogrom in which Jews of Iraq, including my grandparents, were dispossessed, murdered, and raped, was inspired and directed by Haj Amin al-Husseini. He frequently traveled to Germany, rubbed elbows with Hitler, and was as much of an ally of the Nazis as Mussolini was. Al-Husseini was a Palestinian Arab nationalist and the grand mufti of Jerusalem from 1921 to 1948 in British-ruled Mandatory Palestine, where he had whipped up the local Arab masses to brutally attack Jewish civilians, most infamously in Hebron in 1929.

One reason you may not have heard much about us is that the most commonly told stories about Israel don't really take us into account. We are the blind spot in every narrative about our country—including those stories that Israelis have been telling themselves. For decades, we were dismissed by the Ashkenazi elites as a primitive variation of the Arabs who have always been the country's big "other."

We're largely missing from the Zionist depictions of Israel in the Diaspora too. These stories were always centered on the Israel of David Ben-Gurion and Golda Meir and Yitzhak Rabin and Shimon Peres, all Ashkenazi Jews who pumped out a Eurocentric view of the country. As a result, we're often missing from all the talking points about anti-Zionism and antisemitism and the other rhetoric of the pro-Israel community, which is always bending over backward to show how Israelis are *just like* Americans, when in fact we're not.

This is highly unfortunate because we Israeli Mizrahim are the largest demographic of Jews of color in the world. We didn't grow up with privilege, White or otherwise. We suffered intense discrimination in our countries of origin—and still do in many ways today in Israel. We have darker skin and hair than most Ashkenazim. We are not "White" by any definition. But that's not the primary concern. In Israel, the real issue is that our unique customs, experience, and worldview are the very qualities that have caused so much of our hardship.

Outside of Israel, however, what we endure is far worse than the discrimination and microaggressions we suffer at home. Instead, it's a sense of complete denial. Jews deny us; non-Jews deny us.

The prevailing feeling outside of Israel is that *we are invisible.*

Why is this so? Put simply, it's because the Mizrahi identity not only violates the accepted narratives about Jews and Israel, it threatens them.

If you think Jews are a secret network of secular Leftist globalists going after your guns and religion and unborn children, it turns out that Mizrahim are actually fairly Right-wing and pro-religion. If you think Israel is a European, White-supremacist, colonial enterprise that appropriates Arab culture, it turns out that Mizrahim, who are neither European nor White, are the biggest force behind Israel's politics and culture. We were the ones who infused Israeli cuisine with hummus and Mediterranean flavors, not because we wanted to imitate anyone else, but because it was our own culture. We brought it with us to Israel, just as surely as the European Jews brought their whitefish and bialys to New York. If you think all Jews are the beneficiaries of White privilege, it turns out that Mizrahi Jews aren't any more White, physically or socially, than the other Middle Easterners who make this claim.

This is my story. A story of a person with a rich, self-confident identity who, in many ways, has been made invisible in the global conversation about Israel. Yes, I'm also gay, nationalist, proud, progressive, and, of course, Jewish. But the thing about me that really upsets people—what took me years to understand—is that by simply *being* Mizrahi, I am a living, breathing challenge to everybody's pet narrative about Israel.

Perhaps if it were only I who felt this way, this book would just be a memoir. I would probably be somebody's token in the endlessly shallow bickering about Israel. But it's not just me. Being Mizrahi is much deeper and more significant than the endless fights about peace and colonialism and the occupation. It's the story of a real ethnic group, of significant size and influence, that has gone almost entirely unrecognized in the English-language conversation. And without hearing our story, you can't really understand the truth that underlies everything you've read, heard, and talked about when it comes to Israel and Jews.

One way to understand what's missing in today's conversation is to think of Leonardo da Vinci's *Vitruvian Man*—the famous depiction of a man with superimposed positions of his arms and legs. When you see all the ink on paper, it shows the proportions of the human body with genius precision, through sixteen different positions in which this man might be standing. Today's discussions about Jewish identity and Israel are like only seeing the man in one position. Perhaps you can draw conclusions from this singular image, but you cannot give an informed account of its real meaning.

Without knowing about Mizrahi identity, you can't appreciate the beauty of the Jewish image as a whole, or the glorious variations that are available to you. My heritage is the story of a unique culture that has a great deal to contribute to how we understand our Jewishness, our humanity, and our place in the world.

But to even get started, we need to go back more than five hundred years.

2.

THE
MIZRAHI
STORY

I could start telling the story of Mizrahim by going back to 1500 BCE with a history of the earliest Jews and their neighbors on the eastern coast of the Mediterranean Sea, the Nile River, and Mesopotamia. Or I could start with the story of the Jews who built the ancient Israelite kingdoms, in the very land where I began writing these lines, a meeting place of the ancient seats of civilization—the deserts of Arabia, the Fertile Crescent of Babylonia and Assyria, the Mediterranean islands, and the highlands of Asia Minor.

I could start with the time of the Second Temple, when Jews—all of whom were likely brown Middle Eastern people dressed in ancient robes—dedicated their lives to worshiping our God in Jerusalem.

As much of this Jewish history is well documented in scripture, literature, and archaeology, it might actually be more productive to start elsewhere: the Atlas Mountains.

The Atlas Mountains stretch across northwestern Africa, covering about 1,500 miles including modern-day Morocco, Algeria, and Tunisia. These mountains, beautiful and immense in nature, run along the Atlantic and Mediterranean coastlines, with their backs to the seething Sahara Desert to the east and south.

Although ruled today by authoritarian Arab regimes, the Atlas Mountains were once home to free people, most notably the Amazigh tribe, before the Arabian invaders conquered North Africa in the late seventh century CE. Though some refer to the Amazigh as "Berbers," this term is considered derogatory, as it was originally used by Europeans to label the Amazigh as "barbarians."

Women of the Amazigh were particularly powerful back then, revered for their strength and leadership. Unlike the patriarchal societies that characterized most of the world at the time, and still do today, the Amazigh tribes viewed women as queens and goddesses, and many women held active roles in politics and society at large.

Queen Dihya (also called al-Kahina), who ruled during the seventh century, was one such Amazigh war leader. Some of the most complete descriptions of Dihya has been published by Ushi Derman of Tel Aviv's Museum for the Jewish People:

In Muslim sources she is described as "dark-skinned with lots of hair and huge eyes."[1] Fascinated by her exotic image, historian Nahum Slouschz described her as "fair as a horse, strong as a wrestler, a true desert woman, healthy and fast on her feet, an excellent rider and a shooter who never misses," and studied her character throughout Northern Africa. Slouschz asserted that Dihya meant "Jewess" and that "al Kahina" referred to the family of Kohanim (priests).

Queen Dihya was born in what is today the West African nation of Mauritania to a Jewish Moorish Amazigh tribe, and "was the descendant of a priestly family deported from Judea by Pharaoh Necho" more than a thousand years before, during the reign of King Yoshiahu, (around 600 BCE). Dihya succeeded Caecilius as the war leader of the free Amazigh tribes in the 680s CE, leading the battle against the invading Arab armies, and ruled a free Amazigh state stretching from the Aurès Mountains to the oasis of Ghadames from 695 to 700 CE.

When it came to conflict, there were few who could get the better of Queen Dihya. One of her most significant foes was Hassan ibn al-Nu'man, a top military commander for the caliph Abd al-Malik, who occupied much of North Africa at the time and converted large populations to Islam by the sword. In 687, he marched his forty-five thousand soldiers toward the Tunisian capital of Carthage with the intent to seize control. Despite his military prowess, he was no match for an army of Amazigh soldiers led by a warrior queen.

When the Muslim soldiers arrived in her people's land, Queen Dihya first offered peace. However, the caliph rejected, and urged Dihya to accept his authority and convert to Islam.

With no intention of leaving a legacy as a leader who was in command during yet another displacement of the Amazigh tribe, and she certainly did not intend to convert to Islam, she responded that she'd rather perish in defense of her people than give in to the caliph's commands. Inspired by her refusal to back down, Amazigh tribes from across the region joined Queen Dihya, a war they ultimately won. Derman describes what happened next:

> Defeated and ashamed Hassan had to escape with what was left of his troops to Tripoli, where he had to face the Khalif and tell him of his defeat. Al-Kahina chased Hassan's troops all the way to Carthage, and then became the city's ruler.

> Owing to her "Officer and Gentlelady" ethics, she set free all the war prisoners she had captured, except for one: Haled ben Yazid, whom she adopted as her son, on top of her two other sons, one Berber and the other Greek. Apparently, Dihya was no innocent lass. Slouschz wrote she had three husbands forced to satisfy her intense needs, and that she was

"addicted to the lusts of the flesh with all her youthful flaming temper."

This wasn't the last run-in that Dihya would have with Hassan, as Derman describes:

> It took Hassan five years to recover from the losses caused in the battle with Dihya. In the second round, al-Kahina got the lower hand, as Hassan had this time a much larger force. He managed to conquer Carthage and to defeat the Berber rebels. According to Eli Eshed, editor of "תוברת מוקי" magazine, in addition to all her virtues. al-Kahina also had the gift of foreseeing the future, therefore she knew she was going to be defeated and advised her sons to cross the lines and join the Muslims. She herself would not surrender, and used a scorched-earth policy, ordering her warriors to leave no crops, possessions, or livestock, wherever they retreated.

> After her defeat, al-Kahina took her own life by falling into a deep well. The Muslims pulled her body, severed the head and sent it to the Khalif. The well is called up until today "The Kahina Well."

Today, that well is known as the Kahina's Well, or Bir al-Kahina, and is located in the Aurès Mountains in northwestern Tunisia.

Queen Dihya spent most of her life fighting for freedom and her people's religion, and to this day she remains a significant figure in the history of the Amazigh people. And while the Amazigh considered her a hero, stories of Queen Dihya reverberated throughout the world as many groups sought to lay claim to her legacy. As Derman concluded:

> The Muslims said that after her defeat she converted and used her as a classic Muslim role model.... And even the French compared her to their national hero, Joan of Arc, who fought the English and similarly to Dihya was eventually conquered by her enemies.

> The character of [Queen] Dihya also inspired members of the Jewish resistance in Algiers under José Aboulker, whose mother, Berthe Bénichou-Aboulker, wrote a play about the Jewish heroine. Other literary works were composed after Kahina, for example Pierre Benoit's "Atlantida," about a queen heading a Berber lost tribe and turning her lovers into living statues. Dihya is also mentioned in an episode of the t.v. show "Xena: Warrior Princess." It is disappointing that in Israel her story is hardly ever mentioned, with one exception: author Limor Sharir dedicated a few chapters in her book "Secrets of Marrakesh" to Dihya. But mostly she remained unknown.

Queen Dihya's story of defending her people's freedoms and religion inspires me. Perhaps she's where I got my fighting spirit, being that we're both perceived as underdogs who do not give in easily. Given my Tunisian-Amazigh Jewish background, I could even be a descendant of Queen Dihya.

I often find that when my mind wanders, I catch myself dreaming about harnessing the spirit and courage of Queen Dihya to defend my grandparents when they were forced out of Tunisia and Iraq. It's these very thoughts that keep me going at times when I feel overwhelmed or defeated in my charge to tell the Mizrahi story.

Two thousand years ago, a few decades after the time of Jesus, the Jews lost their ancient kingdom in Palestine. A series of political blunders and ill-considered rebellions against the mighty Roman Empire brought destruction on Judea. Over a seventy-year period in the first and second centuries CE, the Romans sacked Jerusalem, burned down the temple, executed the top rabbis, and sent Jews who lived in the region scattering around the world.

However, the Jews didn't disappear entirely. Instead, they reinvented themselves as a people living perpetually in exile, nomadic in how they moved from country to country as the conditions demanded. For a few centuries, they stayed in the Middle East, within major centers in modern-day Iraq and northern Israel. After the rise of Islam in the seventh century, most Jews in the region fled to Europe—mainly to France and Spain—where they stayed until the sixteenth century when Catholic persecutions, the Inquisition, and expulsions of Jews made Jewish life there impossible.

Although Jews had been living in different kinds of communities for centuries across the Middle East, Europe, and beyond, this is really when the big divide began between Ashkenazi and Mizrahi Jews. The Jews of France moved east, creating expansive communities first in the Netherlands and Germany, then in Poland, and eventually in Russia, Lithuania, and Ukraine. These Eastern European Jews became the ancestors of most of the Jews living today in North America, Great Britain, and Europe.

A smaller number of Jews left Spain and migrated southeast, first to Italy, and then to North Africa, Palestine, and the Muslim countries to the east including today's Lebanon, Syria, Iraq, and Iran. There they joined the remnants of more ancient communities—some of which dated back to biblical times—and became known collectively as Oriental or Eastern Jews (the word *Mizrahi* means "eastern" in Hebrew). In these Arab and Muslim lands, Jews were forced to live separately from the dominant Muslim populations and were treated as second-class citizens. Over the centuries, Mizrahi Jews developed their own traditions, Jewish law, culture, food, and even their own languages like Ladino, Judeo-Arabic, and Judeo-Tamazight.

Fast-forward. In the 1940s, as the Holocaust was unfolding and the State of Israel was being founded in Palestine, many Arab countries declared war—nct only on Israel, which declared its independence in 1948, but on their own Jewish populations as well.

Across the Muslim world, Jews were beaten, robbed, raped, and dispossessed. By the hundreds of thousands, they were forced to flee their homelands with only the clothes on their backs. In just a few years, more than eight hundred thousand Jews from Algeria, Morocco, Libya, Egypt, Tunisia, Lebanon, Syria, Iraq, and Iran became refugees. They left behind centuries of history, along with wealth, businesses, property, established communities, memories, books, and traditions.

Many of them, including my grandparents on both sides, fled to Israel.

On my father's side, my family traces our lineage to the indigenous Amazigh people of North Africa. Little is discussed of this group of Tunisian Jews, even though the people were also victimized in the Holocaust and forced into labor camps under the Vichy regime. As a result, the persecution and suffering of Mizrahim in North Africa during the Holocaust is rarely recognized with the same intensity as what happened to Ashkenazim in Europe.

During my last visit to Yad Vashem, the Holocaust remembrance museum in Jerusalem, I did stumble upon a small exhibit dedicated to North African Jews, which noted that fifty Tunisian Jews were killed during the Holocaust. Though I glossed over it at the time, I've since learned that there were periods during 1942 and 1943 when Tunisia was under direct Nazi occupation.

In fact, close to five thousand Tunisian Jewish men, including my grandfather, were conscripted to almost forty detention and forced labor camps where conditions were horrific. Even after being worn down by the Allied forces, German authorities continued to persecute the Tunisian Jews. So while Yad Vashem reported the death toll for Tunisian Jews to be fifty, the number is in all likelihood closer to seven hundred, according to the historian Haim Victor Hayoun, who conducted a 2017 study about Tunisian Jews in the Holocaust.

In May 1943, the one hundred thousand Jews of Tunisia had a reprieve, as the Nazi-backed Vichy French powers withdrew from the country. However, hostility toward Jews there never ended, even after the Nazis left. When Tunisia declared independence from France in 1956, antisemitic laws were enacted that prevented Jews from holding any institutional power and prohibited Jewish gatherings including religious, cultural, and sporting events. In 1958, the Tunisian authorities banned rabbinical institutions altogether and destroyed the traditional Jewish quarter in the capital city of Tunis.

Thus began a period during the 1950s in which the descendants of the ancient Jews of Judea, including my North African Jewish Amazigh grandparents, returned from their centuries-long exile in Tunisia to Israel.

While these Jews were fleeing immense oppression, the journey to Israel was equally formidable. One of the most memorable stories my father told me involved my family's escape to Israel by boat. When my uncle—my father's older brother, a child at the time—fell ill, the ship's captain ordered my grandmother to throw him into the sea. Determined to do anything to save her child, she hid in the bottom of the ship, shielding him under her clothes until they arrived in Israel.

When my grandparents arrived and were asked their family name, they probably thought the question was about the tribe to which they belonged. Their answer was, most likely, "Amazigh" (which literally means "freeman"). I believe that's how I became Hen Mazzig; my ethnic background inscribed in my own name.

On my mother's side, my family came from Iraq, which in ancient times was called Babylonia.

The Tower of Babel is among the most famous biblical stories. Appearing in the early chapters of Genesis, in the Old

Testament, we are taught that at the time, "the whole earth had one language and the same words."[2] The early descendants of Adam and Eve, we are told, built the city of Babel and set about to build a tower attempting to reach heaven. Troubled by their hubris, God scattered humanity into many different languages and cultures. "Therefore its name is called Babel, because there the Lord confused the language of all the earth; and from there the Lord scattered them abroad over the face of all the earth."[3]

The Tower of Babel keeps reappearing in modern cultural references. In *The Hitchhiker's Guide to the Galaxy*, the "Babel fish" is introduced as small, yellow, and leech-like, an oddity that feeds on brainwave energy from those in its proximity. It absorbs all unconscious mental frequencies to nourish itself and allows its user to speak any language they wish. More recently, in her hit 2020 single "Babylon," Lady Gaga sings about the gossipers of our world and refers to the ancient Babylon where all language was lost. Even Marvel Studios placed Angelina Jolie, Salma Hayek, and their fellow superheroes in Babylon for a large part of the 2021 comic book film *Eternals*.

For the Jews of Iraq, however, Babylonia takes on a much more urgent, central meaning to our identity. The great majority of the world's Jews descended from people who lived there at one point or another. In fact, the word *Jew* refers to the

Judeans who were exiled in Babylonia after the destruction of Jerusalem in the sixth century BCE. While many went back to Jerusalem after Babylonia was conquered by the Persian Empire decades later, many others remained. They formed the core of a community that would later become the main Jewish center for centuries after Jerusalem was destroyed again, in the first century CE, by the Romans. The main parts of the Talmud, which is the core of ancient Judaism during rabbinic times, were written in Babylonia. Some of us even stayed there all the way until the modern era, when it turned into what we know now as Iraq. And while some still call themselves Iraqi Jews, many—my grandmother included—prefer "Babylonian Jews."

Indeed, decades after the ancient city of Babylon and the kingdom of Babylonia had ceased to exist, the Jewish community from this region and around the Diaspora continued to use the name Babel to designate Mesopotamia, the "land of the two rivers."

At the entrance to the Babylonian Jewry Heritage Center in Or Yehuda, a large mural of people crying by a river gets its title from a verse in Psalm 137 in the Old Testament: "By the rivers of Babylon, we sat down and wept."[4] The Judeans in Babylon wept over the destruction of Jerusalem and over their exile that would continue for so many centuries on end, until the time my mother's parents returned.

The painting is by Ephraim Moses Lilien, the famed art nouveau illustrator and printmaker whose art on Jewish themes made him one of the first modern Zionist artists.

Ephraim Moses Lilien's mural *By the Rivers of Babylon,* **1910.**

As beautifully painful as this image by Lilien is, it is almost unknown compared to his other work. The most iconic image of the Zionist movement, a 1901 photograph of Theodor Herzl leaning over the balcony at Hotel Les Trois Rois in Basel, Switzerland, was taken by Lilien.

Notwithstanding Herzl's incredible work launching the modern Zionist organization that led to the creation of the State of Israel, the story of Babylonian Jewry and its connection with Zion has never been told in full. Though the passage in Psalms became popularized in Western culture in the early 1970s, first through a Rastafarian song by the Jamaican reggae group The Melodians in 1970, and then through Don McLean's song "Babylon" on his famous 1971 album *American Pie*, awareness of the special resonance it has for Iraqi Jews is far more limited.

For us, Psalm 137 is a foundational text, and worth quoting at length. The first lines describe the sadness of the Israelites in exile, weeping and hanging their harps on trees. Asked to "sing the Lord's song in a strange land," they refuse: "By the rivers of Babylon, there we sat down, yea, we wept, when we remembered Zion. We hanged our harps upon the willows in the midst thereof. For there they that carried us away captive required of us a song; and they that wasted us required of us mirth, saying, Sing us one of the songs of Zion. How shall we sing the Lord's song in a strange land?"[5]

Babylonian Jews see this passage as encapsulating much of their story.

The lines that follow are read at every traditional Jewish wedding, and have come to resonate across the Zionist movement and among Jews of all stripes. "If I forget thee, O Jerusalem, let my right hand forget her cunning. If I do not remember thee, let my tongue cleave to the roof of my mouth; if I prefer not Jerusalem above my chief joy."[6]

And so, Babylonian Jews wept and waited to return to Zion from this foreign land. They passed down this tradition of acute longing, through countless generations, all the way until the middle of the twentieth century, when they finally came home.

In 1951, around the same time that my father's parents arrived from North Africa, my mother's parents came to Israel from Baghdad, Iraq. My maternal grandmother, Hela, who is still alive, is a loving, generous, caring Jewish woman. Despite the unforgettable, overwhelming persecution my family endured in Iraq, she doesn't talk a lot about it.

Instead, she focuses on happy moments. She describes a day in May 1941 when her friend, a young Muslim woman, brought over a plate of sweets for the Jewish holiday of Shavuot. My grandmother fondly recalls their beautiful relationship and her love for her Muslim neighbors. She tells me stories about how gorgeous Baghdad was, how she loved it there, and how they always felt safe, even as a minority.

That was until two days of sheer horror: June 1 and 2, 1941, known today as the Farhud. To me, this event signifies the days of catastrophe and the start of a *Nakbah* ("catastrophe" in Arabic) that very few want to acknowledge or confront. In a matter of forty-eight hours, my family went from being *dhimmis*, a "protected" minority, to refugees in their own country.

Farhud is an Arabic word that refers to the brutal intimidation of a population by its ruler. When asked about life in their former country, Israel's Iraqi-born Jews acknowledge two eras: before the Farhud, and after it. According to my grandmother's stories, the Farhud was much more than just intimidation. It was a level of cruelty that cannot be captured in words.

When she does find a way to express it, she talks about it in the context of the café where she liked to spend her afternoons. It was a beautiful little shop with no front door, just an opening facing the street.

As she sat one day sipping tea with her Muslim friend, she heard an Iraqi Muslim man roaring, "Kill the Jews!" She then spotted her mother's friend, a Jewish woman, walking across the street with her seven young children.

Suddenly, the man pointed a gun at the woman. But instead of shooting her, he began shooting her children. One by one, they were murdered as their mother cried out. Only after he had massacred all of her children did he turn to take her life as well.

The café owner swiftly hid my grandmother in the back of the kitchen. She waited there until my great-grandfather came to get her. In shock and disbelief, they fled back home.

That night, she couldn't sleep. How could she? As her family hid inside her Muslim neighbor's home, terrible noises rang out from the streets. Screams. Sobs. Shattering glass. These were the sounds of lives being stolen. Amid the mayhem, my grandmother overheard her father speaking to the neighbors about which of his Jewish friends had been killed. Recognizing some of the names, she cried herself to sleep.

When morning came, the family was relieved, assuming that the horrors were over. They were wrong.

At noon, my grandmother sat on the balcony of her home while her mother was out shopping for groceries and her father visited a neighbor. Suddenly, she saw Dalia, a mentally disabled Jewish teenager, walking down the street. She called out to her from above, urging her to go back inside. Dalia didn't react.

Within minutes, an Iraqi Muslim man approached Dalia. When he realized that she was mentally disabled, he began to rape her. My grandmother, paralyzed by shock and panic, witnessed the attack, unable to help as Dalia yelled out in terror. When the man was done, he broke a glass bottle in half and shoved it into Dalia's genitals.

My grandmother was inconsolable, unable to speak to anyone about the barbarism she had witnessed. Though she survived the bloody massacres of those two days, a piece of her died that summer. The Farhud reminded her, and all Iraqi Jews, of "their place" within Iraqi society.

Things were never the same after the Farhud, a moment of infamy that marked the beginning of the end for the Jewish community that had lived in Iraq for thousands of years. Most of Iraq's Jews, 150,000 in all, left for Israel within a few years of the massacre, and a small number were lucky enough to move to Britain and the United States. Only around six thousand Jews remained in Iraq.

My grandmother once told me that her father was hanged for being a "spy" (read: Jewish) in the early 1950s in Iraq. When I asked her about it in preparation for writing this book, she asked me not to include it. There is much confusion in my family about her father's death. I also heard other stories about what happened to her father, but I think the trauma is a major cause of fear. She asked me, "Will the Iraqis find out about this book?" and even asked my uncle if it's safe to publish it. It breaks my heart that my grandmother has lived with this fear all of her life, that even the stories of the violence my family endured are not told or even documented.

Another significant blow was dealt to what was left of Iraqi Jewry in 1969 when nine Jewish men from Baghdad and Basra were rounded up and accused of spying for Israel. A hasty trial resulted in a verdict of execution, a public event for which crowds were encouraged to gather and cheer. The Baghdad hangings closely followed the Ba'ath coup of 1968, a time when Saddam Hussein was president Ahmed Hassan al-Bakr's right-hand man. That day, the Israeli parliament held a moment of silence in their memory. Prime minister Levi Eshkol said that they had approached heads of state, religious authorities, and even the United Nations secretary-general to intervene with the Iraqi rulers to reverse the sentence, but to no avail. US secretary of state William P. Rogers condemned Iraq's actions as "repugnant to the conscience of the world."[7]

By contrast, the Soviet Union's official radio network called the executions "fully justified,"[8] while Charles de Gaulle of France said the brutal hangings could not be divorced from the broader Arab-Israeli conflict, as if to imply that these Iraqi Jews were merely casualties of a war happening hundreds of miles away. Rebutting its critics, the Iraqi government-sponsored radio station, Baghdad Radio, said with contempt that while they had hanged spies, the Jews had crucified Christ.

Of course, now we understand that the true motivations behind these hangings were nothing more than a well-orchestrated antisemitic campaign. According to Kanan Makiya in his 1989 book, *Republic of Fear: The Politics of Modern Iraq*, the subsequent international pushback and negative publicity surrounding the hangings had "less to do with the activities of a Zionist lobby as the Ba'th [Ba'ath] claimed, as much as it was the outcome of the deliberately public nature of the proceedings. Later the Ba'th [Ba'ath] learnt the art of sealing out the outside world."[9]

The persecution of Iraq's Jews continued after the spy trials, as described by David B. Green writing for *Haaretz* in 2014: "By the time of the August executions, 51 Jews had been killed by the regime in 1969 alone; 100 more were imprisoned or tortured."[10] In the early 1970s, nearly all of Iraq's remaining Jewish population left after being permitted to do so. A tiny number stayed behind, primarily those who were too old to travel.

The Farhud in 1941, in other words, was just the first step in what was to become the violent expulsion of Iraq's Jews, the confiscation of their property and possessions (valued at an estimated $300 billion), and the erasure of Iraqi Jews' fundamental human rights and dignity.

My family, on both sides, were among more than eight hundred thousand Jews from the Middle East and North Africa who were forced to leave the region following the rebirth of Israel. Maybe because it happened around the same time as the Holocaust, or maybe because Mizrahi Jews are politically invisible, the expulsion of so many Jews from Arab lands is barely known in the Western world, even to Jews. But for my family and for Mizrahi Jews, it is the defining truth of the twentieth century and the trauma our community carries with us, collectively and individually. But the truth remains: there were more Jews expelled from Arab countries than there were Palestinians who left Palestine during Israel's War of Independence.

This fundamental lack of knowledge about the Mizrahi experience, and our own collective voicelessness in the global conversation about Jews and refugees in the twentieth century, has come at an unbearably high cost for us.

I have always been powerfully struck by the similarities between my parents' family stories of discrimination, oppression, dispossession, and ultimately expulsion at the hands of Arab Muslim regimes that never saw Jews as equals. Two different countries, one in North Africa and the other in the deserts of southwestern Asia—with nearly two thousand miles between them—yet far too similar to ignore. This is the Mizrahi story.

Yet there are many circles today, including those of highly respected scholars, in which this story is, simply, denied. Both non-Mizrahi and non-Jews have argued that "Mizrahi" should not be used as an umbrella term, as each community that was expelled from the Middle East and North Africa has a unique story and culture. Of course, each community had its own unique experience—just as every community in Europe experienced its own version of the Holocaust. I don't know any Mizrahim who make the claim that understanding the collective Mizrahi experience should come at the expense of their more specific former national identities as Moroccan, Libyan, Syrian, or Iraqi Jews.

To downplay our *collective* experience, however, serves no purpose other than to erase it. Too many Mizrahim feel invisible in discussions of modern Jewry, and to insist on dividing their experiences is just another tactic aimed at making sure they keep feeling that way.

And yet, when we do attempt to celebrate our collective history through institutions like Mizrahi Heritage Month, we discover Jewish studies scholars like Arie M. Dubnov and Lior Sternfeld dismissing Mizrahi identity as a fabrication, a form of Israeli government propaganda.

But Dubnov and Sternfeld are far from alone. They belong to a critical mass of Western scholars who are trying to rewrite the history of my community. Aided by a few assimilated Arab nationalist Jews and cheered on by virulent anti-Israel activists like Linda Sarsour, they have carved out a new narrative in which Mizrahi Jews are actually just "Arab Jews." This intellectually dishonest pursuit attempts to culturally separate national groups by asserting that each was assimilated into their specific Arab countries, the very countries that oppressed them. Ask yourself, if you were persecuted by your own country—forced to live apart, dispossessed, murdered, and ultimately expelled—would you claim that country's national identity first over all others? Would you ever consider talking about the Holocaust the same way, saying that Europe's Jews were "really" just Russians, Poles, and Germans—when in fact they were specifically targeted by a murderous political ideology simply because they were Jews?

Such attempts to deploy scholarship in the cause of dismantling the Mizrahi identity deliberately weakens every group of Jews who suffered in Arab lands. These actions force us to fight for our rights and dignity in silos rather than as a collective with similar objectives flowing out of a collective experience.

With this understanding, however, it makes sense why our detractors pump out such an absurd telling of our history, for it supports the central narratives of their political agenda: that Israel, the ultimate villain, was founded as a White-supremacist country to oppress indigenous Arabs of color, who are the ultimate victim. There is nothing more inconvenient to the political mobilization against Israel than the discovery that the Jewish state actually is made up of a majority of Jews of color who were refugees from murderous Arab regimes.

But we do not have to submit to it. We can simultaneously celebrate the national heritage of the countries we came from and advocate for our collective story. We can reclaim our place in Jewish history, in the history of the horrors of the twentieth century, and in the Jewish communities of the twenty-first. We can reclaim our dignity, and give due honor to what our forebears endured and dreamed of.

------◆------

The Jews of Arab lands were never "Arabs."

The Arab world as we know it today is the byproduct of modern Pan-Arabism, a political movement that began before the fall of the Ottoman Empire and has roots in the Arab empires of the Middle Ages. In the 1950s and '60s, Pan-Arabism was revitalized by Egyptian president Gamal Abdel Nasser. His policies, which encouraged Arabization programs in Algeria and Iraq, were adopted by Saudis and other Gulf leaders who disguised them under a veil of Arab unity.

The identity description of the "Arab Jew"—though not historically used by Mizrahim—has been bandied about by self-proclaimed anti-Zionist Mizrahi intellectuals such as Ella Shohat and Zvi Ben-Dor Benite, professors of Middle Eastern and Islamic studies at New York University. Shohat and Benite, both of whom live in the United States, claim that they are actually in exile from Iraq, while also rejecting Zionism and Israel because, as they frame it, Zionism is racist against Mizrahim.

Shohat made it clear in her book *On the Arab-Jew, Palestine, and Other Displacements: Selected Writings of Ella Shohat* when she noted how speaking about the history of Mizrahi Jews is erasing Palestinian history. She writes: "Culturally Arab and religiously Jewish, Arab Jews were caught up in the contradictory currents of British and French colonialism, Zionism and Arab nationalism."[11]

Benite similarly made it clear in a 2015 interview for the Alternative Information Center that "regardless of the language and regardless of the culture, saying today that you are an Arab Jew is saying the most subversive thing that you can say against...one hundred-year-old Zionist activity, culture, and propaganda in Palestine, and then in Israel it's very, very strong, which tries to erase their past." He added that "Zionism was imposed on those Arab Jews."[12]

What Shohat and Benite don't seem to understand, or have chosen to ignore, is that by branding themselves as anti-Zionist Arab Jews, they are actually embracing an Arab nationalist and imperialist identity that has been used as the basis for subjugating not just Jews but many other ethnic minorities as well. While generally accepting of the Jewish religion, Arab nationalists vehemently reject Jewish collective identity and political power.

While they can personally identify however they want, it's important to understand how disconnected their views are from those held by the overwhelming majority of Mizrahi Jews, especially those in Israel. Despite the difficulties we and our parents faced in the absorption camps of the 1950s and the discrimination from the Ashkenazi elites that ran Israel until the 1970s, Mizrahi Jews are, by and large, Israeli patriots and Zionists. In order to justify their fantasy narrative, Shohat and Benite have to ignore the historical reality that many Mizrahi Jews were Zionists long before the establishment of Israel. And while some Mizrahi Jews, like the Christians in the Middle East, had friendly relationships with their Muslim neighbors, they lacked anything close to equality, and were often victimized throughout their history in the Muslim diaspora.

They like to paint Jewish life in Muslim lands like a lost paradise, when in fact it was a lot more like the Jim Crow South.

The story of my family, and the Iraqi Jewish community as a whole, is a prime example of Jews' dhimmi status in Arab and Muslim countries. In Iraq, despite being nominally equal citizens, Jews like my grandmother and her family experienced protracted and at times daily oppression, of which the Farhud was merely the climax. For centuries, Jews in the Middle East were legally forbidden from riding horses, building synagogues as high as mosques, bearing arms, testifying against Muslims in court, moving freely after certain hours, and at times dressing without imposed Jewish symbols. In fact, the Nazis got the idea of forcing Jews to wear a yellow star from the rulers of ninth-century Baghdad. This was not limited to Iraq or Arab countries. Prior to the Pahlavi Dynasty's rise to power in 1925, Jews in Iran were considered *najis*, or "unclean," and forced to live in ghettos. They were even forbidden to touch merchandise at a market or go outside when it was raining, out of fear that the water would wash their impurity onto the feet of Muslims.

When, in the 1950s and '60s, radicalization ramped up in North Africa and the Middle East among Arab nationalists who could not tolerate any political power other than their own, Jews across the region were expelled. This was explicit in newly formed nations like Algeria; in 1963, their National Assembly called for a "Muslim Algeria" and voted 85–33 to strip their Jews of citizenship. Those refugees, many of whom joined relatives who had left decades earlier, built cities and neighborhoods like the Kurdish Jewish community in Jerusalem and the Yemenite Jewish community in Tel Aviv. Having sacrificed nearly everything they had to return to their ancient, indigenous homeland, they built and defended new communities in Israel.

So, to those who insist that Mizrahim are just Arabs of Jewish faith brainwashed by the Zionist conspiracy, the only answer is: No, we are not Arabs. We never saw ourselves that way, and no less importantly, the Muslim Arabs who lorded over the countries of our exile never saw us that way. We are Jews, we were oppressed, and we longed for Zion.

But perhaps the most baffling aspect of these anti-Zionist scholars is how they completely invert their own understanding of imperialism and colonialism when it comes to Israel and its Arab neighbors. The founding of Israel is based on protecting a national identity, while the formation of the Arab world began with the Arab conquests of the seventh century and took its twentieth-century form in the "Arab Revolt." This period was the creation of both pan-Arab and pan-Islamic regimes, dedicated to crushing all other identities, including indigenous ones, across the region.

This starts with spoken language, which can tell you a lot about a particular empire or nation. Arabic, like English and French, is an imperial language that was promoted through Arab colonialism and imperial hegemony throughout the Middle Ages. Since the twentieth-century rise of Pan-Arabism, its leaders have pushed Arabization policies on indigenous groups. Whether it be the Kurds, the Amazigh, the Sudanese, the Copts, or the Maronites—none of whom would have called themselves Arab—Pan-Arabism has sought to permanently reduce the status and power of indigenous religious groups across the region.

You would never know this from hearing the words of certain "progressive" scholars. For them, it turns out that imperialism and colonialism are evil when carried out by Western Christian states and empires. Their blind spot for the imperialism and colonialism of the Arab world is a feature, not a bug, of their worldview, a deception that makes them something other than the principled progressives they pretend to be. Over and over again, they choose to neglect oppressed minorities across the Middle East while actively promoting Arab imperialism. Granted, such causes are hardly as popular—or lucrative—as the Palestinian Arab narrative, which is fueled by massive funding from certain Gulf states and especially Qatar. The oppression of other minorities at the hands of Arab regimes is of literally no interest to them—in part because it may draw unwanted attention to the oppression that goes on in the Arab world today.

It is important to note, as well, that these self-proclaimed experts never try to correct the record by using the term *Arab* to describe any other ethnic minority in the Middle East. They wouldn't, for instance, make reference to such groups as Arab Kurds, Arab Assyrians, or Arab Copts.

This is for the simple reason that neither Kurds nor Arabs think that the Kurds are Arabs. But as with so many other things, the rules (of logic, of respecting identity and lived experience, or of intellectual honesty) don't apply when Jews are involved.

Copts, the ethno-religious indigenous Christian group that lives today mainly in Egypt, fought back against Arab imperialism by underscoring their pre-Arab identity. They saw themselves as direct descendants of the ancient Egyptians and their language as a bridge linking them to their roots in a civilization that spans over six thousand years. As a result, they have been brutally oppressed in Egypt.

Many, including myself, point to Bishop Thomas of Cusae and Meir as having offered the most compelling statement about the Coptic identity during a 2008 speech at the Hudson Institute:

If you come to a Coptic person and tell him that he's an Arab, that's offensive. We are not Arabs, we are Egyptian. I am very happy to be an Egyptian, and I would not accept being "Arab" because ethnically I am not. I speak Arabic. Politically now, I am part of a country that was Arabized and politically I belong to an Arabic country, but that doesn't make a person Arab.[13]

He elaborated by saying that if a person believes he is an Arab, his "main focus is the pan-Arab area," meaning he'd no longer belong to the Egyptian nation. The bishop continued:

> You are in or out, you belong or you don't. And this is a big dilemma that is happening for the Copts who kept their Christianity, or rather, say that they kept their identity as Egyptians with their own culture, trying to keep the language...the music...and the calendar of the Copts. That means the culture issue of the old Egypt is still carried on...a process of Arabization has been ongoing in this country for many centuries, since the seventh century.... At the same time, Islamization as well is a dilemma that started and is still carrying a lot of the problems. So when we hear the word "Copt," that doesn't mean only "Christian," it is Egyptian.

The story of the Copts, the Assyrians, the Kurds, the Amazigh, and all indigenous minorities in the Middle East is the story of the Mizrahi Jewish community. We have faced immense pressure from the Arab empire to convert to Islam and accept a pan-Arab identity in exchange for equality. And while a tiny fraction of Jews may have accepted this contrived, colonial oppressor identity, nearly a million Jews suffered as second-class citizens for decades just to stay true to who they were.

Another part of the twisted conversation around Mizrahi identity that has become inverted by activists and self-styled experts concerns the issue of "indigenous peoples." In their attempt to politically tie the Palestinian cause with oppressed peoples such as Native Americans, they frequently paint the Arab population of Palestine as indigenous to the land, and the Jews of Israel, including the Mizrahim, as colonial oppressors. But is this really the case?

The central narrative of Judaism is the story of national liberation of Middle Eastern people from imperial powers. The entire Bible is about a small people's struggle to maintain its sovereignty—ultimately ending in failure—against the empires of Egypt, Assyria, and Babylonia. Resisting imperial oppression is the basis of the Jewish holidays of Chanukah, Passover, and Purim. But it's not just a story from long ago. The liberation of Jews from the crushing fist of empires has actually occurred in living memory, and this reality is crucial to understanding the Jewish story, including the story of Israel. No matter how many wish to craft an alternative narrative, the truth remains that Israel is home to a group of indigenous people who reclaimed their land and revived their ancient language even as they faced waves of violent assault from hostile forces near and far, from Nasser's invading armies to the oppression of Jews in the Soviet Union.

Thousands of years of historical writing and over a century of archaeological excavations have confirmed beyond doubt that the beginnings of Jewish people were, in fact, in the Land of Israel. Due to conquests and imperialism, ethnic Jews have been exiled from their ancestral homeland and subsequently settled in every corner of the world, from the eastern reaches of Russia and China to the Peruvian Amazon. The people who came from Judea are referred to as Jews, even by people who think we do not belong there. Even adversaries like Hamas and Hezbollah do not dispute our right to call ourselves Jews—or, in Arabic, *yahud*.

But as the indigenous rights movement grows, the meaning of indigeneity has become more nuanced. Indigeneity means a tie to a land and a place, thus *indigenous* recognizes this type of connection as originating and belonging to a land. Even some who don't deny the geographical history of Jews are often hesitant to call us an indigenous group, and the effect of all this is to erase yet another pillar of our identity as Jews: our connection to our ancient homeland.

It seemed to me that the best way to understand this issue would be to speak with a member of another indigenous group. So I sat down with Mahrinah Shije, a Sephardic Jew and indigenous advocate belonging to the Tewa people of the

Northern Rio Grande Pueblos. Shije is a development consultant with Zia Impact and a United Nations NGO (nongovernmental organization) representative who also serves on the National Ethnic Coordinating Council of the Democratic Party in the US.

The following section is adapted from my interview with Shije for a *Newsweek* article I wrote on October 15, 2020.

"Judaism is a land-based agricultural religion," Shije told me. "We have had a spiritual and stewardship relationship with the land of Israel since the beginning of our collective memory. Land relationships and stewardship are a critical foundation for any tribe's indigeneity."

Shije draws her definition of indigenous peoples from the United Nations, which defines the term as "inheritors of unique cultures who have retained social, cultural, economic and political characteristics distinct from those of the dominant societies in which they live."[14] She noted how indigenous peoples have sought recognition of their identities, lifestyles, and rights to ancestral lands throughout history. Yet their rights have continuously been violated by empires, nation-states, and external colonial powers.

Any Jew in the past thousand years who has chanted "Next Year in Jerusalem" during a Passover Seder can understand this. "I will add that indigenous peoples must practice a land-based tribal religion," Shije said. "Whether Jews want to acknowledge it or not, our religious practice is both land-based and agrarian, additionally sharing our tribal history across a cyclical lunar calendar."

As a member of both communities, Shije has experienced firsthand how Pueblo People and Jews share ritual practices of giving thanks for the food, land, knowledge, and other gifts from our Creator. In particular, she believes that what Jews do every Friday evening, by welcoming in the Angels of Peace to mark the beginning of Shabbat, resembles customary native rituals of welcoming spirits or ancestors.

Shije believes that all Jewish holidays—Sukkot in particular—have customs that resemble those of other indigenous cultures. For example, all Native American groups orient themselves among their sacred directions, just as Jews pray toward Jerusalem. They also ritually utilize species, the way Jews wave the *lulav* and *etrog* on Sukkot. "We, as indigenous people, pray in the ways and languages of our ancestors as much as we are able. Jews do too."

When it comes to the question of Israel, the answer is clear to Shije: "We are indigenous to Israel because it is our ancestral homeland, home to the history and accomplishments of our people, the bodies and blood of our ancestors."

Shije believes that one can indeed lose indigenous identity, but not by living in the Diaspora. "If they became a different identity and are no longer Jews, then they're no longer indigenous. They're whatever they became," she said. "If they don't pray for Israel, feel themselves a part of our people (in the greater sense—past, present, and future generations), or have relationships with our ancestors there, if they don't identify with our tribe, then they're not."

As an advocate for indigenous peoples, Shije takes issue with how anti-Zionists have tried to compare Palestinians to Native Americans. According to her, pro-Palestinian activists have visited numerous tribes in America to argue that their narratives are the same. "They are not," she said. In effect, she explained, pro-Palestinian activists are co-opting the indigenous experience for their own political gain. She believes American Jews should be owning their identity as indigenous peoples and building relationships with analogous communities.

"Jews are not only indigenous to Israel—we are Indigenous Peoples. We must remember that," she added. "Look into Native communities around your area, learn about them and their needs—connect with them. Understand how similar we are as Indigenous Peoples, and how we must work together."

Shije said she speaks particularly to Jews who live in the Americas. "Native American battles for sovereignty, language reclamation, traditional food production, water protection, ecological preservation, religious expression, and defining our modern realities through our own cultural lens not only reflect the same struggles and accomplishments of the Jewish people, but also positively benefit Jewish lives in the United States."[15]

One final point before getting back to my story. As more and more people outside of Israel learn about Mizrahi identity, the question is increasingly raised: What's the difference between "Mizrahi" and "Sephardi," the more traditional English-language term for non-Ashkenazi Jews?

The two terms have different lineages and meanings. "Sephardi" refers to *sefard*, or Spain, in Hebrew. The word refers primarily to the Jews who left the Iberian Peninsula in the wake of the Portuguese and Spanish Inquisitions in the fifteenth century and ended up mainly in the Middle East and North Africa. In traditional Jewish speech, it also refers to their form of Orthodox Judaism, which is similar to Ashkenazi Orthodoxy but has its own special variations in practices, legal rulings, and prayers that emerged in the centuries that have since passed. Many of the most influential rabbis in the Middle East over the last few centuries carried with them ritual traditions that originated in the academies of Spain, and many of the oldest Jewish communities in the United States were founded by those who had gone west instead of east when they left Spain or Portugal—ending up in the Caribbean before finally settling in New York in the eighteenth and early nineteenth centuries. For all these reasons, the term *Sephardi* came to describe the bulk of the non-Ashkenazi world of ritual, synagogues, and communities centered on religious tradition.

Mizrahi, or "Eastern," is a newer term, but it refers to a more ancient phenomenon. It comes from the older term *Adot Hamizrah* ("communities of the East"). It is more cultural-ethnic than religious, and it recognizes the fact that Middle Eastern Jews were not all expelled from Spain and Portugal; indeed, many of them had lived for millennia in the Middle East—not only well before Jews arrived from Iberia, but also before Islam was founded and the Arab adherents of Muhammed rampaged across the region, conquering and converting by the sword.

So, while the two terms enormously overlap, there are some key differences. An ultra-secular Israeli whose parents came from Iraq, where they had lived for at least a thousand years, probably won't identify much with the label "Sephardi." At the same time, a descendant of expelled Spanish Jews whose family went west instead of east, will more likely call herself Sephardi rather than Mizrahi. And so, as you can see in the 2021 Pew Research Center study of American Jews, 3 percent call themselves Sephardi, and another 1 percent call themselves Mizrahi.

But because our whole story is about ethnicity and shared historical experience, not religious practice, and because I'm not an especially observant Jew, I have always seen myself as

Mizrahi, as do more than half of Israel's Jews. If someone asks me, "Are you Sephardi?" I'm likely to say, "Well, yes, that too."

In a meeting I had with Shmuel Trigano, a renowned sociologist and professor emeritus at Paris Nanterre University, he argued that we should actually drop the term *Mizrahi* and instead identify as Sephardi. According to Trigano, *Sephard* is a biblical term that is actually the most accurate way to refer to our community.

Certainly, there is a wealth of evidence showing how interconnected the Sephardi and Mizrahi labels have been. One of the most well-known Mizrahi Jewish scholars was Moses Maimonides, who grew up in Spain but lived most of his life in Egypt and Morocco, where he wrote some of the central religious texts Jews still study to this day. Broadly, there was a vibrant relationship between the Jewish communities of the Middle East and those of Iberia, as many Jews had moved back and forth between them for centuries prior to the expulsion of Iberian Jews in the late fifteenth century.

But while I agree with Trigano on his presentation of our community as having a shared history and identity, I firmly reject the choice he makes about which label to prefer. Of course, everyone is free to identify as they choose, but I think there are good reasons to prefer Mizrahi, a cultural-ethnic term that describes our shared history dating back to the Islamic conquests of the seventh and eighth centuries, rather than Sephardi, a religious term dating back to the fifteenth.

We are much more deeply united by our experience under Islamic rule than by minute differences between our religious practice and that of the Ashkenazim. Being a non-observant Jew who is descended from Amazigh and Babylonian Jews, calling me Sephardi feels, simply, wrong.

Another distinguishing factor between the two terms is language. Mizrahi Jews are not united by a single "Jewish" language. Each subgroup spoke its own tongue—some combination of Arabic or Middle Eastern language and Hebrew (much like Yiddish blends German and Hebrew, and Ladino is a Spanish-Hebrew combination). So I continue to find it odd when traveling in the Diaspora and I encounter a Sephardi person, who you think would understand these complexities, and he or she starts speaking to me about Ladino. As Jewish as the Ladino language may be, I've had little experience with it, even though many assume the opposite. I grew up hearing my Iraqi grandparents speaking Judeo-Iraqi Arabic, and my Tunisian grandparents speaking Judeo-Tamazight. Ladino is as foreign to me as Yiddish.

Hopefully by now you can understand that today many Jews live a multilayered existence, especially in the last half century and especially in Israel. Some Sephardi Jews attend Hasidic yeshivas, and some Mizrahi Jews enjoy gefilte fish on Passover (don't ask me why). One of the most amazing things about Israel has been the way Jewish communities have merged and intertwined, driven by a high rate of internal intermarriage, especially in the last generation. Jews from all backgrounds are known to exchange each other's cultural traditions. And as Jewish communities grow and diversify, we've seen a range of ethnicities even within individual families. This is true even in a place as homogeneously Ashkenazi as the United States. Indeed, in that same Pew Research Center study, fully 6 percent of American Jews reported being "some combination" of Ashkenazi and Sephardi or Mizrahi—in other words, more than the percentage saying they were Sephardi or Mizrahi combined.

As a result of this increased multiculturalism within the Jewish community, I often hear Diaspora Jews use this as evidence to conclude that the cultural divide between Mizrahim and Ashkenazim has largely been blurred and become meaningless.

This is not the case, however.

When I was growing up in Israel, we learned about the atrocities of the Holocaust told solely from an Ashkenazi perspective. Our school curriculum never included details about the history of my family. While every Israeli knows who Mizrahim are, the relative lack of Mizrahi perspective in Israeli education is still an open wound today.

Economic disparity between Mizrahim and Ashkenazim also still exists in Israel. Mizrahi Jews came to Israel with minimal property and little to no wealth, and this deficit has continued throughout the last several decades, resulting in extreme inequality and lack of representation in almost every area of public life today.

What we need, and what the Jewish community deserves, is an unbridled telling of the Mizrahi experience throughout history—our struggles, our triumphs, and our goals. In the Diaspora, and especially in North America, the basic reality of Israel as not just a Jewish state but also one that is heavily Mizrahi—and what this implies about the culture, politics, and inner need for a Jewish state—must become deeply ingrained in the story we tell ourselves about Israel. The global Jewish community will not be completely whole until our story becomes an integral part of every Jew's story.

I am a Jew, an Israeli, and a Mizrahi. And if you cannot see me for who I am, you will forever misunderstand what Israel has become, and you will be forever limited to a tragically narrow view of what being Jewish can be.

COMING OUT, TWICE

"What do you want to be when you grow up?" As I remember being asked this throughout my childhood, I have an even stronger memory of my consistent response: "I want to be Ashkenazi."

This answer, just five words in length, encapsulated much of the first twenty-five years or so of my life. It revealed a complicated mixture of shame, fear, rejection, and a desperate longing to be accepted.

My home life and school life consistently felt at odds with each other. In many ways I was living a double existence. Though I often reflect fondly on childhood moments like when my grandmother played records by Egyptian singer Umm Kulthum, I can't help but still feel the humiliation I experienced when my third-grade teacher, an Ashkenazi Israeli, laughed at me when I told the class that my favorite musical artist was an Arab. My classmates, even the other Mizrahi kids, laughed along as the teacher quipped, "Oh, these people have no culture."

Later that day, when I told my grandmother what had happened, she laughed and issued her classic retort: "Your Ashkenazi teacher is telling you we have no culture? What culture does she have?"

In all likelihood, my teacher had a wonderful culture, which you could read about in any number of books about the founding of Israel as seen from an Ashkenazi perspective. But her inability to recognize my own, and that of half the Jews of Israel, was disheartening.

Instead of celebrating our history, Mizrahim have been made to feel ashamed of it. This not-so-subtle message has been conveyed by most of the cultural gatekeepers who have celebrated the Western and European Jewish identity since Israel's inception. These individuals, along with the institutions they control, have demonstrated a perpetual desire that we Mizrahim assimilate into the "mainstream"—that is, Ashkenazi—culture whose dominance they are charged with preserving. Many share the belief that Israel would be better off if Mizrahim were "a little less Arab."

My internal tension about my identity did not stop with third grade. Three years later, I lied to my Ashkenazi teacher when I told her that I was half Ashkenazi. Without recognizing the complexity of my family's actual background, I went on to tell her that my mother was from Denmark, I had Danish Jewish roots, and I had once traveled there to visit family. I was begging for approval, willing to do or say almost anything to gain a reprieve from the feelings of belittlement. Later that year, when my mother asked me why my teacher inquired about our family in Denmark, I realized that while lying about my sexual identity would be difficult, misrepresenting my family's history would be a far greater challenge.

By the time I graduated from high school, my identity had been firmly shaped by what I saw around me. I did not see myself as Mizrahi. I am Israeli, I'd tell myself over and over again, because we are all Israelis no matter where we come from. Soon after, I would learn that while we are in fact all Israelis, not all Israelis share the same experiences, history, and perspectives.

In my early twenties, one of my closest friends was Nahum, the son of two Israeli Left-wing Ashkenazi journalists. I know this because he reminded me of it whenever we spoke about politics.

"Why do *they* keep voting for Likud?" he'd ask me, referring to the many Mizrahim who supported the more conservative political parties in Israel. "Do they not see how they are harming our country? The bigotry, the discrimination. They are ruining Israel!"

When I'd ask what exactly he meant when he used the word *discrimination*, he'd say, "Against the Palestinians, of course!"

I was as baffled as I was hurt. It felt like my friend was attacking me, albeit indirectly, for the fact that Israel had a Right-wing government.

I did make an honest attempt to engage Nahum in a respectful dialogue about this extremely complex situation. I explained that many Mizrahim, including my father, vote for Likud *because* of the discrimination they have faced since coming to Israel. To be clear, this is not Nahum's parents' brand of discrimination. It certainly isn't the kind of thing you'd read about in their erudite magazine and news articles, composed of words and perspectives that afforded him the kinds of privilege that most people in my community had never known.

I'm not sure if what I was trying to articulate actually ever permeated his worldview. Nor can I be certain it ever occurred to him that while his family owned a massive house in Tel Aviv along with several other homes, my parents were still paying a mortgage for their small two-bedroom apartment in the not-so-affluent suburb of Petach Tikva.

I told Nahum that my father still remembered the days when David Ben-Gurion's Mapai party, the forerunner of the Labor Party, was in power. My father recalled how he was denied countless job opportunities because he was not Ashkenazi. While perhaps not discriminated against solely on the grounds of ethnicity, he did not hold the Mapai membership card that was given to select Israelis, almost all of them Ashkenazim. Instead, and quite proudly, he started a career as a truck driver.

"Hen," Nahum stopped me. "We are all Israelis. Stop making divisions."

I smirked and offered that he lead by example. This was one of my earliest memories of standing up for myself and my community.

Although politics is always a potentially polarizing force, it is bizarre to see the ways that Ashkenazim on the political Left express their hatred for Likud. While I do not share the Right-wing ideology and have been very critical of Likud's policies as well as its leader, former prime minister Benjamin Netanyahu, I can also see the reality on the ground. Week after week through most of 2020, during the height of the COVID-19 pandemic, Left-wing protesters rallied outside the prime minister's residence in Jerusalem. Nahum was frequently among them.

Interestingly, the police officers there to keep the peace—many of whom were Mizrahi and Ethiopian—received the brunt of the crowd's ire. This created a disturbing dichotomy where racism was felt and seen, yet went entirely unaddressed. It soon became clear that the several thousand mostly Ashkenazi Israelis who protested there each week were not objecting to Netanyahu or his policies as much as they were sending a direct message to the voters who put him there in the first place.

In those moments, it no longer felt like a protest by people determined to change the way the government serves its citizens. Rather, it was a crowd filled with angry Left-leaning elitists who, despite their vocal efforts, were not getting what they wanted. Their gripes were glaringly rooted in the unabashed entitlement of Israel's Left, a primarily Ashkenazi force that wants to regain control of the country that was "stolen" from them when Likud rose to power in 1977 and cares little about eliminating actual racism and other forms of injustice. Unfortunately for these elites, Mizrahim in Israel understand when they are being used as political pawns. They would rather vote for Netanyahu, a man who speaks *to* them, even if he fails to serve their best interests, than for the parties of the Left, which purport to be on their side but can't look them in the eye.

Experiences like these colored much of my childhood and early adulthood, but I still can be surprised by how explicit certain Ashkenazi Israelis can be when they think we're not listening. On a sunny Tel Aviv day in 2016, I sat outside a coffee shop enjoying a sesame cookie and a cup of coffee. I happened to overhear a conversation between two older

Ashkenazi men, both vocal Labor supporters. Listening to them was as fascinating as it was infuriating.

Dressed in grubby shorts and T-shirts in the faux-proletarian style of Israeli elites, they were discussing the real estate properties they owned. The conversation took a sharp turn when one of the men, quite unashamedly, expressed frustration with certain tenants whom he called the *frankim* (a derogatory term used to describe Mizrahim). The other chimed in to affirm his belief that Mizrahim "have ruined our country." The first man nodded in agreement, responding, "How I miss the good old days, the good old Israel. When we led this country."

I have no doubt in my mind that they miss the good old days. They probably miss the time before my grandparents left the ma'abarot, when they could control our mobility, both economically and socially. They likely long for the time when my people were more manageable, when we had fewer opinions, fewer voices, and fewer rights.

As awful as it sounds, the Ashkenazi Left in Israel overwhelmingly seem to believe that Mizrahim should just be grateful to be here at all, as one prominent anti-Netanyahu protest leader expressed more than once in late 2020. According to the *Times of Israel*, at one demonstration, former Air Force General Amir Haskel told an Israeli policewoman of Ethiopian descent, "I brought your parents here from Ethiopia, aren't you ashamed of yourself?"[1] This kind of thing is all too common among certain Israelis who lament that Jews of color ruined their dream of a more Western, Eurocentric Israel.

This attitude has contributed to the enduring struggle my people have experienced throughout the last half century. They were expelled from their home countries where they felt they belonged but were never truly "Arab enough for the Arabs." And when they finally got out, Mizrahi Jews made it to Israel, where they may have enjoyed formal equality before the law but were nonetheless made to feel like second-class citizens all over again.

This started early in Israel's history with our founders who, for the most part, built the cultural, economic, and military infrastructure of the new country. They also often saw Mizrahi Jews as "not Israeli enough."

Contrary to what many Ashkenazim believe, though, they alone did not build Israel.

In his 2019 book *Spies of No Country*, Matti Friedman shares previously untold stories of four Mizrahi Jews who were members of a spy unit called the Arab Section for the Haganah, the militia that became the IDF when Israel declared independence in 1948. This unit, composed entirely of Arabic-speaking Mizrahi Jews, risked their lives both inside the territory that became Israel and across dangerous borders in Lebanon and Syria.

The Arab Section trained Mizrahi Jews to pass as Arabs.

What's especially moving about *Spies of No Country* is that prior to independence, members of the Arab Section technically spied for a country that didn't even exist yet. In other words, they sacrificed everything they had for the *idea* of a country that happened to be dominated by European Jews. One has to wonder why—and be in awe of—people who would risk so much for an unborn nation whose self-proclaimed founding fathers were hardly accepting of them and their culture.

What's even more raw, painful, and inspiring about these stories is that until Friedman's book, they'd gone virtually untold, not only in America and the Western world, but even in Israel. For more than seven decades, the complex reality of these loyal Israelis who were challenged and vilified again and again by Ashkenazi Jews was missing from the pages of history books everywhere.

It's not a huge secret that today, in Israel, Mizrahi culture still faces heavy resistance from both Arabs and Ashkenazi Jews. Meanwhile, the situation is far worse elsewhere in the Middle East, where Arab and Islamic countries are actively wiping away the history of the Jewish communities that once lived there.

Prior to 1972, Egypt was home to seventy-five thousand Jews. Today, only a few dozen remain. Iraq's once

150,000-strong Jewish population has met a similar fate, and not one of the quarter-million Jews who once lived in Syria and Libya remain. Most recently, the few remaining Jews of Yemen were forced to leave the country by the Iran-backed Houthi Islamists.

Mizrahi Jews found refuge in Israel, and though we have basic rights, we are still underrepresented in many areas of society. We face continued discrimination, much of it subtle, whether or not our fellow Israelis want to admit it.

Perhaps it's difficult for Ashkenazi Israelis to identify with our plight because today many Mizrahim are fairly assimilated. The Mizrahi Jews who helped build Israel in the 1940s and '50s, on the other hand, did not have the freedom to assimilate in the way my generation did. Not only did Jews like my parents speak Arabic, the language of Israel's enemies, but their culture, attire, and identity were too similar, in Ashkenazi eyes at least, to those attempting to destroy the newly established state.

Gamliel Cohen, one of the spies chronicled in Friedman's book, described the difficulty he had finding a kibbutz that would accept him as a member due to his Syrian origins. When he finally joined one in 1940, he expressed frustration about how some of the *kibbutznikim* acted as "cultural guardians" by repeatedly refusing to allow Arabic music or the public display of any aspect of Arab culture.

It's not lost on me that Gamliel likely enjoyed the same type of music I grew up with and still listen to today. We Mizrahim have our own unique traditions, food, music, and idiosyncrasies, dating back thousands of years.

And yet, for far too long, we've avoided celebrating our heritage openly because, quite frankly, we have internalized the messages coming from a "mainstream" Israel that celebrates Western and European culture without apology.

All our lives, we've been told how lucky we are to even be here. As a result, we've refrained from staking a claim and promoting our contributions.

But times are changing. We will no longer be erased, minimized, or silenced.

ZOHRA AL FASSIYA

Zohra Al Fassiya

was a singer at the court of King Muhammad the Fifth in Rabat, Morocco.

It is said that when she sang, soldiers drew knives, to push through the crowds and touch the hem of her dress, kiss her fingertips and express their admiration with a Rial coin.

Zohra Al Fassiya

These days she can be found in the poor part of Ashkelon, near the welfare office, with the odor of leftover sardine cans...marvelous kingly rugs stacked on a Jewish Agency bed, and she, clad in a fading robe, lingers for hours before the mirror wearing cheap makeup, and when she says: "Muhammad the Fifth, the apple of our eyes" it takes a moment before you realize...[2]

—From *A Moroccan Gift*, Erez Bitton

On the eve of Israel's independence in May 1948, the Israeli Jewish community numbered roughly 650,000 people, a relatively homogenous population that was 80 percent Ashkenazi and 20 percent Mizrahi. In the years that followed, Yemenite Jews, Libyan Jews, and Iraqi Jews all arrived in Israel. After them, in the 1950s and '60s, came the mass immigration of Jews from North Africa and then Iran. Today, Mizrahim constitute 53 percent of Israeli Jews.

Upon arrival, roughly one-third of the new immigrants were sent to special absorption camps known as ma'abarot. The stated objective of the camps was to help immigrants transition from their native country to their new homeland. Though they were designed to absorb immigrants from all over the world, the great majority there were the Mizrahi Jews.

They traveled to Israel on airplanes. For most of them it was their first time ever flying in one. They were forced to leave behind their property and land, which by some estimates was equal to five times the size of Israel today and has a current value of about $300 billion. What you can't put a price tag on, however, is the loss of their culture and their basic human dignity.

The United States, much like most of the world, closed its gates to Mizrahi Jews, making Israel their only refuge. Following the enactment in March 1950 of an Iraqi law that allowed (or encouraged) only the Jewish people in Iraq to forgo their citizenship and leave the country, over one hundred thousand Iraqi Jews left. My mother's parents arrived one year later and were sent to a ma'abara in northern Israel.

On my father's side, my Tunisian grandmother, Kamisa (meaning "luck" in Tunisian Arabic), and my Tunisian grandfather, Benyamin, were sent to Rosh Pina, a town in the Upper Galilee not far from Safed. It was a backwater, with little hope for economic mobility. They stayed there for years.

The living conditions in the ma'abarot, many of which were former British army outposts, were intolerable. The immigrants were housed in large tents, where makeshift partitions separated families from one another. When the tents reached capacity, huts and shacks were built. Toilets and showers were located outside the living areas, and people often had to wait in long lines to use them. The *olim* ate their meals in communal dining rooms. As awful as the ma'abarot were, they were nonetheless provided to these dispossessed refugees free of charge.

Facing difficulties absorbing its new population early on, the state appointed the Jewish Agency, a quasi-governmental body that channels foreign donations to Israel, to provide for most of the immigrants' needs. As the number of the refugees escalated so did the burden on the Jewish Agency. In some camps, food shortages left thousands starving, leading to declining sanitary conditions and disease. The shortage of doctors and medical equipment led to many preventable deaths as well.

Unemployment rates in the camps were extremely high. Finding a job was difficult in Israel in general at the time, but even more so for the Mizrahi Jews of the ma'abarot, who were located far from the bigger cities and were unqualified for most professions. The Israeli government did not make any significant attempt to reverse this trend.

Arye Gelblum, writing in *Haaretz* on April 22, 1949, described the Mizrahi immigrants this way:

> This is a race unlike any we have seen before. They say there are differences between people from Tripolitania, Morocco, Tunisia and Algeria, but I can't say I have learned what those differences are, if they do, in fact, exist. They say, for example, that the Tripolitanians and Tunisians are "better" than the

Moroccans and Algerians, but it's the same problem with them all....

The primitiveness of these people is unsurpassable.... As a rule, they are only slightly more advanced than the Arabs, Negroes and Berbers in their countries....

The [North] Africans bring their ways with them wherever they settle. It is not surprising that the crime rate in the country is rising.... Above all there is one equally grave fact, and that is their total inability to adjust to the life in this country, and primarily their chronic laziness and hatred for any kind of work.[3]

My Iraqi grandmother, Hela, and my grandfather, Abraham, were sent to a camp up north called either Kfar Hasidim or Shaar Haalia. My grandmother still vividly recalls her time spent living in a tent, and later a tin shack. Rain and cold weather made it nearly impossible to sleep in the winter, while snakes and wild animals often paid evening visits to their tent.

Years later, when my grandmother visited the small Babylonian Jewry Heritage Center in Or Yehuda, she wept at an exhibit of a tent that looked eerily similar to the one in which she lived as a young woman. The display immediately brought back many painful memories. She instantly remembered how the beds covered half of the tent's area, and she recalled the beautiful Iraqi dress that she had hung on a string above the dirt floor. Though each family was allowed only one suitcase, she had held onto that dress, the only thing she owned, hoping to one day wear it again.

As the years passed, the Mizrahi immigrants began to move more toward the center of the country. My Tunisian grandparents eventually found a place in an impoverished neighborhood in the city of Lod. Lod was already known as a poor city—and where they were placed, referred to as the "Lod Ghetto," was even poorer. The ancient city of Lod had a significant Jewish community from the second century BCE to the eleventh century CE. In 1948, during the War of Independence, most of the city's Arab inhabitants were expelled from what was at the time known by the Arabic name of Lydda. The town was resettled by Jewish immigrants, most of them from Arab countries, alongside about a thousand Arabs who remained. Today, about a third of the city's seventy-seven thousand residents are Arab.

My father had a rough childhood in Lod. He was beaten up by his Arab neighbors often and regularly went to school with just a piece of bread with some margarine—the only lunch my grandparents could afford to feed each of their sixteen children.

My Iraqi grandparents, on the other hand, were placed in Petach Tikva, at the time a fairly distant suburb of Tel Aviv. They were given a two-bedroom apartment on the third floor and another one-bedroom unit on the fourth floor in a housing project. While it might sound like a lot of space, it was not nearly enough for this family of eleven children.

My grandfather was able to buy land in Petach Tikva equal to one dunam (a quarter acre) when they first arrived in town, but officials from the Ashkenazi-dominated Mapai party convinced him to give back the land in exchange for housing. It wasn't until later that he realized he also had to pay for the apartments if he wanted to keep a roof over his head.

"Your grandfather was a barber and a man who was very afraid," my mother once told me. "He was afraid of the government, of its officials, but he also wanted to do what was best for Israel." When I asked my mother if that experience made him change his mind about the Mapai party, she told me that he still voted Mapai, and later Labor, until his dying day. "He was always afraid of them," she'd reiterate.

The trauma my grandfather carried with him from Iraq exacerbated his continued fears of government officials, which was similarly felt by my Tunisian grandfather. My father, Yakov, has told me about how my grandfather would be furious with him whenever he'd criticize the Ashkenazi-run Mapai. My father explained that the family was generally fearful of Mapai, who called them *shchorim* ("blacks") and used other derogatory terms like baboons, *frankim*, and *chakhchakhim* (mocking how the North African accent sounds to Ashkenazi Jews by emphasizing the *ch* and *kh* when they speak).

It wasn't until Menachem Begin, the famous Likud leader who became Israel's sixth prime minister, entered the public sphere that anyone recognized Mizrahim as a group with shared interests that had been ignored for far too long.

On May 10, 1972, the CIA issued a detailed report called "Israel: Problems Behind the Battle Lines." In 2017, that report was declassified[4] and released to the public. In the eighteen-page document, which can be found on the CIA website in full, its authors spell out the tensions between Ashkenazim and Mizrahim at length. This report is probably one of the most detailed external accounts of the dynamic that was unfolding in Israeli society at that time and provides a fascinating look into the power of Israeli political parties, the rift among different ethnic and religious groups, and the struggles endured by Eastern Jews.

Among other issues, the report dedicates an extended section to the tension between "Ashkenazi" and "Oriental" immigrant groups, and adds a third category, that of the "Sabra," or Israeli-born descendants of immigrants from both sides of the Jewish map. Because it captures so much of what my parents lived through, as seen through the eyes of American observers, that section is worth quoting at length:

12. By far the most important domestic social problem—one with a potential for political instabi-
lity—is the deep cultural, economic, and political
differences between the Ashkenazi and the
Oriental Jews. The only bond between the
Ashkenazi and the Oriental seems to be their
mutual adherence to Judaism and allegiance
to Israel. Great differences exist in cultural
background, education, social values, and even
in physical characteristics. The Orientals, who
often have darker skins, are sometimes referred
to as "black Jews"; they maintain many of the
characteristics and habits of their original non-
Western environment. The Oriental Jew is most
often poor, ill-educated, and has few skills;
he generally has a larger family than does an
Ashkenazi. Most Oriental Jews are latecomers
to Israel (in the 1950s) and are on the bottom
of the socioeconomic ladder; they are not well
fitted to compete in an industrial and basically
Western society.

13. Status and power in Israel lie with the Ashkenazi
Jews and their Sabra descendants. Pioneers from
Russia and Poland were the principal Zionist
activists, the early settlers, and the leaders of
the labor and kibbutz movement. They were, in

short, the dominant figures in the formation of Israel. The Ashkenazim are usually highly literate, European in culture and technological skills, and imbued with the Western work ethic.

14. The overwhelming majority of Oriental Jews are drawers of water and hewers of wood. In 1969 only about seven percent had made it up to professional, scientific, and technical jobs, and only about ten percent were administrators, managers, executives, or clericals. In 1969 the annual income of the Oriental family, while increasing, was still well below that of both the Ashkenazim and the Sabras. As a result, the Oriental is not a large consumer, cannot afford adequate housing and most often lives in the big-city slums. He finds that higher education is almost entirely reserved for his European or Sabra neighbors. Enrollment in high schools and universities in Israel is based on performance in competitive national examinations, which put Oriental students at a disadvantage. Moreover, higher education is expensive. Both high schools and universities have tuition fees. Many of the Oriental students who do enter high school drop out before graduation.

15. Although the Ashkenazim are in the driver's seat now, the Orientals have outnumbered them since the early 1960s and are growing more rapidly than the other two groups. An estimate made by the US Embassy in 1965 indicated that by 1980 the balance between Ashkenazi and Oriental Jews might be on the order of 35-65 percent. This has raised concern among the Ashkenazim that in time their influence will be diluted and that Western-oriented Israel might ultimately become another Levantine state.

16. Though a community of over one million people, the Orientals do not yet appear to be organized politically. They are spread through several political parties from left to right. In the October 1969 parliamentary elections, the Young Israel Party, which perennially runs on the specific platform of increased influence for the Orientals, won a minuscule 2,000 votes out of 1.36 million votes cast—not enough for one seat. Of the 120 members elected in 1969 for the current Knesset, only 13 are Orientals; there is only one Oriental in the 18-man cabinet (the Minister of Police). The Orientals are heavily represented in the police force, but at best have only token representation in the rest of the civil service. There are two Chief

Rabbis, one Ashkenazi and one Oriental. Mrs. Meir's Labor Party in June 1972 named a Yemeni Jew, Yisrael Yeshayahu, as secretary general of the party, apparently to underscore its awareness of the problem. Yeshayahu has since been Speaker of the Knesset.

17. The apparent widespread apathy of the Orientals and their inability or unwillingness to act as a unified political force have stemmed in part from their basic conservatism, but they may be becoming more aware of their political potential and majority position. In the spring of 1971, a small group of Oriental youths, calling themselves "Black Panthers," staged a series of public demonstrations in Jerusalem and Tel Aviv. With an assist from some splinter Communist groups, they protested discrimination against Orientals in housing and jobs and brought the plight of the Oriental Jews to public attention. They were particularly disturbed that the new immigrants from the Soviet Union (most of them Ashkenazim) and other Western immigrants were being given priority in jobs and new housing. Recently an Oriental leader was quoted as saying, "If we ever get peace in the Middle East, we will have civil war at home." Another likened the situation to that of Ulster,

comparing the Catholics in Northern Ireland to the Oriental Jews in Israel as the large-family, low-paid class of society, and the Protestants to the Ashkenazi Jews, "who have the power and large incomes."

18. These statements may be overblown, but the discontent is real, and the problem probably cannot be indefinitely set aside. The government is trying to bridge the gap between the Orientals and the Ashkenazim. The major effort is directed at recasting the Oriental in a Western mold— mostly through Hebrew language training, special educational benefits, agricultural and other vocational training, and army service. But progress is slow, both because of the nature of the problem and because of limited finances. The government will have to run hard just to keep ahead of the Orientals' rising expectations. The eventual assumption of power by the Sabras could bring an evolutionary solution—there seems to be less awareness of "differentness" among younger Israelis.[5]

While this report is soaked with the kind of racist overtones we can expect from early 1970s classified CIA prose, especially when talking about other countries, it nonetheless describes a lot of the realities that my family, and more than a million other Israelis, faced back then. We were a majority of the country, yet we felt like a permanent underclass without real access to the levers of power and wealth in the country.

The document is also prescient in its description of the coming political upheaval. Just five years after it was issued, in 1977, Menachem Begin led the Right-wing Likud party to electoral victory, and he became prime minister. For the first time, the movement of Mapai-Labor, which had led the Zionist movement for more than half a century and had ruled the country since its founding in 1948, was out of power.

Begin did it by channeling the same Mizrahi discontent that the CIA report talks about. But we didn't wait for an "evolutionary solution." The 1977 victory was nothing short of a revolution.

Begin, of course, was himself Ashkenazi. As were most of the Likud leaders. As was much of the Herut movement he had led, the precursor to Likud, since 1948. As had been the Irgun underground militia he had led against Ben-Gurion's much larger Haganah during the pre-independence era. As had been his mentor, Ze'ev Jabotinsky, and the Revisionist movement he had founded to counter Ben-Gurion as far back as the 1920s.

The Likud leadership was almost as Ashkenazi as Mapai and Labor had been, but Begin was different in a crucial way: He respected Mizrahi Jews, and he respected Jewish tradition, whereas Mapai was an elitist, socialist, arrogant Western movement, looking to build a new world disconnected from anything having to do with the life of the shtetl in Eastern Europe. And because Begin respected tradition, he could speak to the largely traditionalist Mizrahim too in a way that no Israeli leader had done before. Call it populism if you will. But for the first time, Mizrahim felt that Israel was truly their home only when Begin came to power.

Four years later, in the June 1981 elections, this clash inside Israel came to a head. Begin was looking for reelection, and everybody wanted to know if the 1977 victory had been a one-off or represented a fundamental shift in how the country would be run—and by extension, the status of Mizrahim in Israel.

The final campaign rallies for the two big parties, Labor and Likud, took place on consecutive nights just a couple of days before the vote in Kings of Israel Square in Tel Aviv, which is today called Rabin Square. The first night, when Labor had its rally, comedian Dudu Topaz was one of the speakers, and in a moment reminiscent of Hillary Clinton's 2016 "basket of deplorables" speech, he used the term *chakhchakhim* to describe the Mizrahim who were supporting Likud.

Begin's response, delivered on the same stage the following night, was a seminal moment in the history of the Mizrahi role in Israeli life. Here is part of what he said:

Last night, in this plaza stood a young actor—what's his name? Dudu? Dudu To-paz. Dudu Topaz. He said here the following things. Now, there was total quiet, so that you couldn't hear a fly, absolute silence as one hundred thousand people of the Labor Alignment listened to Dudu Topaz. He said the following words: "The *chakhchakhim*, they're at [Likud Headquarters] in Metzudat Zeev. They are barely guards at the base, while here—meaning last night—stand the soldiers and officers of the combat units."

I must admit before you, that until this morning I had never heard the word *chakhchakhim*, and I didn't know what it meant. In the Underground, during the period of the Revolt, [Hagana commander Yisrael] Galili asked me... when we were planning operations together against the British, he said to me the following words: "How did you solve the problem of the *Adot Hamizrah* in the Irgun?"

And I looked at him, baffled, and I said to him, "Yisrael, what are you talking about? What problem?"

And he said: "Come on, you know, haven't you heard? The problem of the *Adot Hamizrah*."

So I said to him: "What problem? We have no problem. We are all brothers, we are all Jews, we are all equals—

all of us!... The great commander of the provinces—a Yemenite! Uzi was Sephardi. Gidi, who did the historic operation at the King David Hotel, was Sephardi. The commander in charge of all the prisoners at Latrun was Yemenite, and all our young men stood before him at attention. What problem? We had none."

We are all Jews! We are all brothers! We are all warriors!

But listen, when that guy—what's his name? Du-du To-paz—when he said that stupid, idiotic thing, those wicked words of his, the whole audience that stood here, last night—they applauded and cheered....

Will every hired actor speaking for the Labor Alignment stand up and commit blasphemy? The people of the *Adot Hamizrah* are among the greatest warriors of the IDF. They—together with Arik Sharon—crossed the Suez Canal and went to the other side. He commanded them, among the best of Israel's warriors! And now someone will say before the vast throngs of the Alignment, cheering and applauding, what did he say? "*Chakhchakhim.*" *Chakhchakhim*, that's what he calls them....

Never has such blasphemy been uttered. Never has anyone tarnished the honor of an entire tribe of

Israel, as did the Labor Alignment last night, in this very place.[6]

Begin was an incredible orator. He spoke from the heart and connected with each and every Mizrahi Jew, somehow bringing out the fire of thousands of years of collective Jewish history, and Jewish honor, in every word.

This speech was probably what made the difference in the 1981 election, as Likud won by just a single parliamentary seat. With only a few exceptions in the 1990s, Israel has been governed ever since—for better and for worse—by leaders who came out of Begin's national movement, while Labor has been reduced to a minor party, winning just seven seats in the 2021 election.

"You don't know what it meant to us," my father told me, "to be recognized for the first time as equals and not ignored, unfairly treated, or dismissed because we are not Ashkenazim. Of course I vote for the Likud—they gave me everything I have. We had nothing before they took office. I will never forget it."

It was extremely difficult for my father to get a job in Israel. Add to it the fact that Lod lacked a proper education system, and that he'd often have to delay his studies in order to find odd jobs to help his parents make ends meet.

Even when he was drafted into the Israel Defense Forces at eighteen, he did not have the same opportunities that Ashkenazi Israelis had. One's assigned role in the army was based on one's *Kaba*, or quality group ranking, a system that was used as a first cut to evaluate the likely contribution you could make to the military. The Kaba was based on a wide variety of parameters that included level of education, socio-economic status, performance on psychometric exams, and a personal interview. If you lived in Lod, your ranking was low. If you were poor, it was lower. And if you had eleven siblings that had to be cared for, it was even lower. I can't say for certain that this ranking system was intentionally designed to oppress Mizrahim in particular, but it was unequivocally the result.

My father became a truck driver, the profession the IDF assigned him and which he would continue to make a living from until the 1977 Israeli elections.

My father hated the fact that his skin color and ethnic background prevented him from fulfilling his potential. My mother, Cami, on the other hand, had a little more luck. Iraqi Jews, and specifically those from Baghdad, were considered to be "civilized" Mizrahim. While similarly unworthy of equal treatment and subjected to racism both blatant and subtle, they were given opportunities in banking due to their involvement in financial businesses in Iraq before they arrived in

Israel. It makes sense, then, that my mother worked for many years at an Israeli bank.

That bank, called Bank Hapoalim ("the Workers' Bank"), was established by Mapai in 1921 and still exists. Though it was created with the intention to serve the "workers" in Israel, it functioned just like every other institution in the country, benefiting mainly Ashkenazim who were the only ones working in white-collar professions.

I still think about the times when my mother would come home from work in tears, scrambling to find the nearest Hebrew dictionary. She'd pull a note from her pocket scribbled with words in Hebrew that she didn't know. This was a point of anxiety as her bosses at the bank would mock her poor Hebrew.

I hugged her tightly as she learned the words, and she'd say, "Hen, you must promise me you will go to school and finish. Never be like us." It was at that moment I promised myself that I would do everything in my power to be *exactly* like them—brave, resilient, and tenacious.

As I was growing up, my family lived paycheck to paycheck. On more occasions than I can count, my mother asked me to take her card to the bank to withdraw small sums of money from her account. Time and time again, her card was declined. Today, she still tells me about how heartbreaking it was for her not to be able to provide for her kids. Even her and my father's combined salaries were rarely enough to get through the month.

The cues I got from my family were similar to those coming from society at large. Much like being gay, being Mizrahi was something to be ashamed of, something I'd have to disguise if I wanted to fit in properly. For most of my life, I put on several fake personas. Just as I'd put on a masculine act in an effort to hide my queerness, I tried to behave like how I thought Ashkenazim would, masquerading as someone I wasn't in order to feel a sliver of societal acceptance.

When I turned eighteen, I joined the Israel Defense Forces for mandatory military service.

Following my initial processing and Kaba evaluation, my options were immediately limited. They told me I could either be a truck driver, a soldier supporting artillery, or a member of what was called Coordinator of Government Activities in the Territories, or COGAT. As I wanted to make the most meaningful contribution I could, the first option did not seem ideal. The second one, to be a combat soldier, did not appeal to the humanist in me. The third option, however, was intriguing. As I looked more closely at the details of COGAT, it became clear that I wanted to join this unit.

Charged with managing all civil aspects in the parts of the West Bank that are not under the direct rule of the Palestinian

Authority, COGAT is responsible for overseeing the construction of medical facilities, schools, environmental projects, roads, and water-related infrastructure. It also coordinates with the Palestinian Authority's security forces, with the goal of minimizing the conflict's impact on civilians.

The unit's mission, in other words, is in every respect humanitarian in nature, aimed at easing life for ordinary Palestinians and de-escalating difficult situations. It is not especially popular among young Israelis. Very few Israeli teens, traumatized by decades of war and terrorism, feel compelled to serve their country by helping civilians on the other side.

In basic training, we learned about the Oslo Accords and the different systems operating in the West Bank as a result. We studied Arabic too, which was easier for me than for my peers. My grandmother still speaks Arabic with her children.

When I completed my training, I was placed in the international organizations department of COGAT due to my command of English. And so, at eighteen, I found myself on a bulletproof bus heading from Jerusalem to a military base in Ramallah, where I was sent to work with Palestinian civilians. It was a strange experience for someone who not only understood how violent regimes oppressed my family in Iraq and Tunisia, but also grew up during the second intifada, the

broad campaign of Palestinian terrorism that included horrific suicide bombings in the early 2000s. I was just twelve
when I survived a terror attack, so the fact that I was now on
a bus heading into a Palestinian town to help its Arab civilian
population weighed on me.

Upon arriving at the base, I was assigned to a dorm with
six other male soldiers. My roommates came from all walks
of Israeli society. To say this was challenging for a closeted
gay Mizrahi kid who also had body issues would be an under-
statement. I'd often shower only after all my roommates had
gone to bed, or I'd wake up at 4:00 a.m. to shower before
they got up.

Looking back, I understand that I was holding too many
secrets inside for far too long. While I was home on leave, a
good friend of mine came out to me as a gay man, and my own
anguish became unbearable.

These feelings accompanied me throughout my service
as a soldier in Ramallah and carried over when one of my
commanders told me he thought I should go to the officer
training course. I was young, overweight, and hated exercis-
ing, so the thought of spending eleven months in a very masculine environment with tough field conditions was daunting.
But being an officer in the IDF is a badge of honor in Israeli
society, especially for young, elite, often Ashkenazi Israelis. I
accepted the challenge.

The course was grueling, but my thirty-year-old commander never gave up on me. He genuinely wanted me to succeed. As we grew closer, he became like a father to me.

And so, for the first time in my life, I decided to share my darkest secret with him. I was terrified about how he would react. But it turned out that, while he appreciated how hard it must have been for me to open up, he frankly didn't give a damn about my sexuality. He reaffirmed his commitment to training me to be the best IDF commander I could be—and then honored that commitment in full.

His belief in me boosted my sense of security and pride, and I started losing weight. Soon I was able to run for more than ten minutes at a time, matching my personal record as a teenager. I started to really feel like I could be an IDF commander. Losing weight was a powerful metaphor for the immense burden of the secret that I no longer carried alone. In the end, the final test in the officers course was a lot easier than I had predicted. I graduated with the rank of first lieutenant.

Still, I didn't tell anyone else I was gay. Though my commander was accepting, I was concerned about what others would think and, most importantly, how my family would take it.

As the liaison officer to the UN and other international organizations, I was stationed first in Jerusalem and later in Hebron—the biblical-era city where the Jewish patriarchs and matriarchs were, according to tradition, buried. The job in Hebron was especially challenging. It's a large and often hostile Palestinian city, with an enclave of highly spirited (some might say crazy) Jewish settlers dedicated to protecting one of Judaism's holiest sites. And my job was to help the Palestinian civilian population there.

In that role, nobody from any side liked me. My UN counterparts viewed me as an occupying soldier, someone they'd have to simultaneously struggle against and need support from. The Palestinian officials did not appreciate my presence there at all, while the settlers saw me as a traitor. And the IDF soldiers positioned to provide security saw me as a distraction. It was then, as I walked into this no-win situation, that I first discovered the universal truth that those who do the most important work are the least appreciated.

Looking back, this was the best preparation I could have had for my career as an activist.

The most challenging aspect of my post was working with the United Nations Relief and Works Agency (UNRWA). This UN body was created in 1949 to support Palestinian refugees, commonly referred to as "generational" refugees because—unlike all other refugees, who are taken care of by a different UN agency, the United Nations High Commissioner for Refugees (UNHCR)—the Palestinians' refugee status is passed down from parents to their children and even grandchildren. It was an awkward feeling to witness the immense efforts being made by the world to serve Palestinians. After all, there was no such UN group set up to help Mizrahi families like mine who were expelled from Arab countries decades before. Yet this feeling of injustice didn't undermine my resolve to do my job as best as I could.

Every human being deserves dignity. And true peace in the region can only be achieved when those on the other side of the conflict have the same opportunities for a good life.

This work also proved especially rewarding because many of the Palestinian civilians I served were—like me—hiding their queer identity.

I remember one Palestinian man, let's call him Ahmed, coming to apply for a permit to enter Israel. He kept coming every day to inquire about his permit, even though we were processing the requests as they came in from the civil coordination officer of the Palestinian Authority, which collected them from Palestinian civilians. On the third day I took Ahmed aside and asked him why he was so pressed on getting that permit. He said that he had met someone online from Tel Aviv, and they really wanted to unite in person. Some people call it "gaydar," but when I asked if his family was concerned about this meeting, his eyes twitched, and he knew what I meant. The following day I had Ahmed's permit approved for six months.

My curiosity about Ahmed's fate continued for a few months, and I checked in our system and discovered that he never returned to the West Bank after crossing the border to Israel. While unlawful, I knew Ahmed was just trying to protect himself and to live freely—neither of which could he do among the violently homophobic Palestinian society. Sometimes I imagine him today, living in a beautiful apartment in Tel Aviv with a new name and a Jewish husband, and I am deeply grateful I could have played a small role in saving him.

My approach was, and has always been, to fix systems and structures that are broken, not to burn them all down in the pursuit of my goals. In Israel, I want to work within the democratic system, and to improve it, because I love the idea of the Jewish state, and I know firsthand that it provides safety to my people. It would be hypocritical for me to not love this country, as it has done so much for my family, and for so many others, when options were scarce. I am confident that I can help change Israel from within, just as I did in the army.

Toward the end of my five-year military service, I did finally come out as gay to my friends, and later on to my family.

I gathered my childhood friends. "I wanted all of you to know that, well, I don't think I'm into girls," I said.

One of my best friends was Regev, and after a brief silence, he spoke first. "And?" he said. It took me a minute to understand he was just accepting me as I am.

"We love you, Hen, but this doesn't change who you are for us," Sagy, another friend, said.

Minutes later another friend of ours, Dean, arrived, and I had to tell him. Dean is our group's comedian, and he replied, "No way!" I confirmed it, and he got this terribly dark look on his face. "Well," he said, "that's awful."

And then he burst out laughing.

I felt so much joy that day because my closest friends all accepted me for who I was. These friendships have continued ever since. A decade later, Regev, Sagy, and Dean are all happily partnered with amazing women, and we are still as strong a group of friends as we have ever been.

If only it were that easy with my family.

There is a stereotype of the Jewish mother who worries about her children so much that every offense is met with a guilt trip. Usually, we assume this is an Ashkenazi thing, but my Iraqi Jewish mother can teach these mothers a thing or two. I took her to a bar in Tel Aviv, feeling like the casual atmosphere would help me come out to her; it wasn't as easy as I hoped it would be. When I finally told her I was gay, she spent the next hour telling me how bad she felt.

Her problem, of course, wasn't that I was gay, but how she felt knowing that I had been in the closet all these years—and she blamed it on herself. "I failed as a mother if you never felt safe enough to come out!" she sobbed. And so I suddenly found myself consoling and hugging her as she reacted to my coming out with an explosive display of guilt. It was sweet nonetheless.

My brother's response, the following day, was that he was so proud of me, and it didn't matter whom I loved as long as I was happy. My brother is as masculine and straight as they come.

Now I had to face my dad. I knew it wouldn't be easy with him, but I also knew it wasn't because he didn't love me or care for me. It was more about how he grew up and the people around him. He responded that it was a hard thing for him to hear, and that he hoped to be okay with it later on. Now, years later, he is excited to meet my British partner, Marc, whenever we come to Israel.

Though my father still grapples with my sexuality to this day, my mother accepts me and regularly reminds me that her love for me is unconditional.

Perhaps the most freeing experience during the entire coming-out process was my first pride parade in Tel Aviv in 2011. Suddenly I was surrounded by thousands of people just like me—confident, unapologetic, and self-aware—and I finally felt true acceptance in a way I'd never before experienced. Most importantly, the parade gave me strength not just to accept who I am, but to take pride in it.

Marc told me after his first Tel Aviv pride parade that it was unlike anything he had experienced. "It is a true celebration of pride, and a riot, fighting for your rights," he said. "By the beautiful beach and the sun above, marching down the road with thousands of people in the Middle East felt so empowering." He also told me how the song "Tel Aviv," by the Mizrahi singer Omer Adam, was his favorite part. This song was written for the parade and became its theme song, weaving together Middle Eastern music and Arabic and Hebrew Israeli gay slang words in its lyrics. Marc remembers how he was surrounded by queer people at some point who were all dancing to the song. He said this was a moment he will never forget.

All of this then got me thinking. There was one more secret I was still keeping inside out of fear of how the world would react.

I would have to come out a second time.

It wasn't until I moved to the United States in 2012, and began working for a Seattle-based pro-Israel organization, that I felt like people were ready to hear my full story.

I had always wanted to move to America. I grew up watching American TV shows and admiring its popular culture. When I finished my military service, I knew I had to find an opportunity to move there, so when this pro-Israel organization posted an opportunity online, I went for it. After a few meetings and public speaking tests, I got the job.

I was hired specifically to speak about how great Israel was to me and my family, and how I was lucky to live in a country where I could be openly gay. The directors of the organization urged me to use my family's story to debunk the anti-Israel claims that Israel is an oppressive White-majority nation hell-bent on oppressing people of color.

Though I agreed with the sentiment, I hated the way I was being told to express it.

I don't know if this is fair, but it's certainly how I felt at the time: I was hired to act as a puppet for an Ashkenazi- and straight-dominated organization trying to earn points in a political debate. The truth is that I wouldn't have minded it as much had I believed that those running the organization actually cared about these issues. However, it immediately became apparent that they only wanted me to speak about my experiences when it helped advance their agenda.

I still remember the racist comments I had to deal with, like the time a senior member of the staff posted online that "Mizrahi Jews are not just sitting around drinking tea all day— look at Hen Mazzig's work!" I assume it was an attempt to flatter me, but it was insulting to think someone at a senior position even held these opinions and was willing to express them in public.

When I suggested the organization help sponsor the pride parade in Tel Aviv, another director denied it. A religious man of British origin, he was constantly calling me out for posts that were not "in line with the organization's agenda." He was referring to my occasional criticisms of Israel's policies. When I spoke about the inequality Mizrahim faced in Israel, another senior member of the team told me that it was best to not confuse young Jews about Israel; just tell them "we're all the same and we are all Jewish." He also said that my talk about the history of Mizrahi Jews in the Middle East must be about how the Arabs forced us out of our lands and Palestinians were removed in a coordinated act of population exchange. That was simply not true, and I could not believe someone would tell me to say it.

I didn't respond well to these demands. I insisted on speaking from a true, personal place. These were my stories and my beliefs. I couldn't then, and I still can't, parrot other people's talking points to serve other people's agendas.

The more I spoke about my family's story, the prouder I felt about our collective experience. My second coming out was well under way before I even knew it.

I started writing articles about my family's stories and traditions as well as the Mizrahi culture and agenda. First, I wrote for local Jewish media in Seattle, which was part of my job, and in which I defended Israel. Later on, I wrote for the *Times of Israel* and the *Jerusalem Post*, now more openly about my complex views. When I'd finished writing one article, I'd write another, and then another.

To express myself, my background, and my life story in an open and honest way without interference was intoxicating. It's an addiction I have yet to kick, much to the chagrin of those who protest my events and call me a murderer.

Of course, Ashkenazi Jews regularly shared my writings to affirm their own political views. Many of them believed either that Israel was above criticism because it saved Mizrahi Jews (the "you should be thankful" crowd) or that Israel must be endlessly criticized because of the its systemic discrimination against Mizrahim.

I didn't care about that anymore, because I just wanted to get the truth out. People needed to know. Today, the story of the Mizrahi Jewish community is being discussed in English-speaking countries more than ever before. I'd like to believe that I've had something to do with that trend, standing on the shoulders of a few great and brave Mizrahim who chronicled this history in Hebrew and French.

Today I try my best to find the nuance in everything I write and share. I am indeed critical of the many inequalities my community faces, but I do not come from a place of resentment or hate. As James Baldwin put it in his 1955 work *Notes of a Native Son*: "I love America more than any other country in the world and, exactly for this reason, I insist on the right to criticize her perpetually."

I too love my country and my people. I love them so much that I pledge to continue improving not only their lives but the very system on which their livelihoods and freedoms depend. In the face of constant criticism and derision, the easiest thing to do would be to lie down and just give up. But I've never been one to take the easy path.

4.

JEWS WILL
NOT ERASE US

A prominent former Israeli politician called me one day in early 2021, after I had begun writing this book. He was familiar with my work and wanted to hear my take on several social issues. The conversation went well until I began talking about this book and my plan to weave my personal narrative as a gay Mizrahi Zionist Jew into the larger framework of Israeli society and Jewish culture.

The response I received was all too familiar: "Don't talk about this issue of Jews of color. It's too divisive and never ends well."

I was troubled, but more than that, I was shocked. Shocked enough to break out of a bad case of writer's block.

As long as I can remember, the idea that talking about Jews of color is somehow toxic has been the default belief across the Jewish community, especially in the Diaspora. This is because the Ashkenazi Jewish identity has been the predominant cultural, economic, and political force not just in Israel, but even more so across the Diaspora and especially in the United States.

Commonly referred to as "Ashkenormativity," this phenomenon has largely rendered Mizrahim and other non-Ashkenazi Jews of color invisible to the communal conversation. It has fostered an unforgiving dichotomy in which Mizrahim, if they are seen at all, are depicted either as low-class people who vote predominantly for Right-wing parties, or far-Left elitists engaging in some kind of self-hatred.

There are Mizrahi Jews who are even more vocal in their criticism than I am, sometimes to a fault. Writing for *Jewish Currents* on this subject in April 2019—the only piece addressing Ashkenormativity to be found on the predominantly Left-wing website—Devin Naar, an associate professor of Jewish and Sephardic studies at the University of Washington in Seattle, calls out what he describes as a "White supremacy" problem within the Jewish community. He sees this as the result of a "chain reaction" flowing from the way Ashkenazi Jews were treated in Europe.

> When Europeans disparaged Jews by analogizing them to two Others in particular, black people and Muslims/Arabs, they set off a chain reaction, whereby European Jews came to displace these comparisons

onto the "fallen" or "fake" Sephardic Jews, subsumed by the Muslim world.

I'm not a fan of this kind of heated, jargon-filled rhetoric, his need to position Ashkenormativity as a form of "White supremacy," with all that it implies, or his virtue signaling to the woke Left. But I can certainly see the merits of Naar's most important point: for a great many American Jews, Mizrahim *are* the invisible "other" that Ashkenazim once were in Europe.

My own philosophy, however, is rooted more in the often controversial idea of intersectionality.

Kimberlé Crenshaw, an American lawyer and civil rights advocate who coined the term, explained this set of ideas in a 2016 TED Talk. "African American women, like other women of color [and] like other socially marginalized people all over the world," she said, "were facing...challenges as a consequence of intersectionality, intersections of race and gender, of heterosexism.... [T]hese social dynamics...create challenges that are sometimes quite unique."

I take this to mean that every group (but minorities especially) faces specific challenges that only they can see and feel. We cannot adequately address these challenges unless we're willing to be open and try to understand the experiences of people in that group, irrespective of our own group's particular needs.

To me, in other words, intersectionality should be viewed as wholly distinct from the concept of identity politics, which has gained prominence due to its propensity to create a dialogue that cuts down certain voices in the name of inclusion, diversity, and justice.

On the contrary, I believe that "intersectionality," as originally formulated, calls upon us to listen to people who have different experiences, and it should never come at the exclusion of others. While I do believe that Ashkenormativity has been a detriment to the Mizrahi people and Jews of color, it shouldn't be so much to ask for a world in which all voices are heard and respected.

This notion is rejected by some of my detractors on the Right, who bristle at the idea that minority voices are worth hearing and understanding. While I have engaged with people of this camp, since I believe I can convince others of my point of view, I understand that intersectionality is a hard sell. It's not a lost cause, but anyway, this is not my core audience.

My detractors on the Jewish far Left—those who preach inclusion and diversity while beating the drum against me and my Zionism—would give you an entirely different explanation as to why this kind of intersectionality can never work. They argue that we cannot listen to Israelis, categorically, as long as "the Palestinians are not free," and that a system built on oppression must be fully dismantled in order to serve marginalized people better. Again, I don't see things to be that black and white. There very well can be a middle ground, but at its root, it must begin from within the Jewish community itself.

In August 2020, I wrote a column for the Los Angeles *Jewish Journal* titled "Are Jewish Institutions Fighting Racism Wrong?" In the article, I commended the many strides that Jewish American communities in particular had made in addressing institutional racism within their ranks. From events to forums to conference calls, it was clear that Jews were willing to have challenging conversations about the discrimination that Jews of color face within their own communities.

Too often, however, these conversations were missing a crucial component: Mizrahi Jews, speaking firsthand about their experiences. Such was the case with Hillel International's "Racial Justice Learn In," an event held earlier that month for the Jewish community to engage in deep introspection about race.[1]

"Given that Hillel—by far the biggest organization dedicated to enhancing Jewish life on college campuses—has such wide reach among Jewish youth. I was excited to see the flagship organization commit to 'building a big, wide tent for this gathering, as we come together to confront white supremacy, learn from many JOC [Jews of color] teachers, and hold up the diversity of our Jewish community,'"[2] I wrote at the time.

Especially as we were in the middle of a global pandemic that saw a resurgence of antisemitism in the United States, to see an event branded this way meant a lot to me. The event was sponsored by several other major Jewish institutions, including the Charles and Lynn Schusterman Family Foundation, the Jewish Multiracial Network, Jewish Women's Archive, Jews of Color Initiative, Keshet, Moishe House, T'ruah, and National Council of Jewish Women.

While Asian Jews, Black Jews, and even those who did not identify as Jews of color led panels about racism, not one of the thirty-five events focused on the Mizrahi experience or Ashkenormativity. This might have been more understandable if Mizrahim were really a tiny population with little representation to be found. However, the case is quite the opposite. There are more than four million Mizrahi Jews in the world, making up over 25 percent of the global Jewish population and more than double the number of Jews in the entire New York metropolitan area.

It is hard for me to cast blame on Hillel while it was trying to highlight underrepresented voices. At the same time, though, the absence was glaring. And it stung.

In reality, many people just don't know anything about Mizrahim, or that we are a group at all. I travel to universities around the world and lead discussions on Jews of Middle Eastern and North African descent. Yet even after speaking with many Jews, they'll tell me that I am the first Mizrahi Jew they have met. When I first heard someone say this, I was blown away—similar, I imagine, to how American Jews must feel the first time they meet someone who has "never met a Jew." Now it actually makes sense to me, considering that Mizrahi Jews often tell me that they feel invisible, both within the Jewish community and even in the very heart of the struggle to make it more inclusive.

Not even having money or being famous makes you immune to this gap in Jewish cultural understanding. We saw this with the incident surrounding the comedic actor Seth Rogen in summer 2020. Appearing on the popular podcast *WTF with Marc Maron*, Rogen made foolish comments questioning the legitimacy of Israel's existence, saying that even having a Jewish state "doesn't make sense."[3] Rogen wasn't explicitly addressing Mizrahi erasure, but his example shows that even well-off Ashkenazi Jews who create public personas as progressive icons have a tendency to look at Israel through an extremely narrow, Ashkenormative lens.

Most Mizrahim see Israel as making a lot of sense, since it's the only reason they can live in freedom today. Imagine how they must have felt listening to Rogen use his massive platform to make jokes at their expense.

I reached out to Rogen after that, and I was grateful that he answered. But he didn't seem to empathize with the plight of Mizrahim or even understand that we exist at all. Despite efforts on my part simply to educate him about a history he wasn't aware of, he continued to push back against every point I made by just repeating, "What about Palestinians?"

This form of evasion, instinctive among many progressive Jews, is just another act of erasure.

Like Rogen, I also have Palestinian friends, and through my work I've helped relocate dozens of LGBTQ Palestinians who are oppressed by their own leadership. At the same time, I was talking about Mizrahi Jews, but Rogen just replied: "I have a lot of Palestinian friends with a perspective I was never taught." This is a microcosm of the challenge Mizrahi Jews face in the Diaspora—the nearly universal inability of non-Mizrahi Jews to hear us. We simply aren't there.

The invisibility of Mizrahim in the Diaspora may seem strange considering how much Israel is discussed. But it makes more sense when you understand that almost everything that comes out of Israel is filtered through the Jewish state's own Ashkenormative lens. In a country where more than 50 percent of Jews are Mizrahi, Ashkenazim are dramatically overrepresented in nearly every sector.[4] In universities, 91 percent of academic staff, 61 percent of students, and all presidents have been Ashkenazi—except one, who was only half Ashkenazi. Of the 221 recipients of the Israel Prize, an award regarded as the state's highest cultural honor, only 20 have been Mizrahi.

Every head of Israel's official theaters has been of Ashkenazi heritage. When it comes to senior judges, 90 percent are Ashkenazi and 9 percent are Mizrahi. Of the ten Israeli state attorneys, not one has been Mizrahi. The same can be said when it comes to the position of the Bank of Israel governor. All eleven heads of Mossad have been Ashkenazi (again, one of them had a Mizrahi parent). Of course, every prime minister of Israel to date has been Ashkenazi.

This also says nothing of the fact that in Israel, which has been dubbed a "start-up nation," Mizrahim are also wildly underrepresented in tech. The only data available on the ethnicity of Jewish entrepreneurs in Israel was conducted by Urginea Ventures in 2013, which found that 78 percent of the Israeli tech entrepreneurs were Ashkenazim.

According to the Adva Center, in 2018, first-generation Ashkenazi men who had immigrated to Israel before 1989 had the highest average monthly salary of ILS 18,772 (if 1 USD is 3.26 ILS, it will be about $5,750). Next were second-generation Ashkenazi men, with ILS 16,483, on average (about $5,056). Below them were second-generation Mizrahi men, with ILS 14,153, (about $4,340) then first-generation Mizrahi men who arrived no later than 1989, with ILS 13,578 (about $4,165). At the bottom, the lowest wage earners were Arab women, Jewish women of Ethiopian origin, and Mizrahi women, with an average monthly salary of ILS 6,674 (about $2,047).

When it comes to representation in popular culture, Mizrahim also get the short end of the stick. Osnat Mark and Miri Regev, two prominent Mizrahi Israeli politicians, are regularly portrayed through an offensive caricature—that "bleached-blonde bimbo aunt" every family has. Even *Eretz*

Nehederet, the wildly popular Israeli comedy sketch show, regularly mocks Regev, a former senior minister, member of the Knesset, and former IDF brigadier general, by highlighting characteristics that liken her to a *frecha.*

Meaning "joy" in Arabic, *frecha* is a Hebrew slang term that in Israel has come to be synonymous with an airheaded Mizrahi woman who sleeps around.

The male equivalent to *frecha* is *ars,* which characterizes Mizrahi men as violent gang member types. These portrayals often enter mainstream culture through outsider interpretations of our music. Famed Israeli rapper Dudu Faruk is one example of someone who represents many of the worst stereotypes of Mizrahi culture. His YouTube videos draw millions of viewers in Israel, with one reaching almost six million views. What makes his persona more cringy and offensive is that he is actually a twenty-four-year-old Ashkenazi.

This leaves us with two possible interpretations of Dudu's act. At best, it could be seen as an honest misinterpretation of Mizrahi culture based on a desire to emulate us and reject his Ashkenazi heritage. At worst, it's an intentional satire that invokes bigotry toward Mizrahim by those who have no broader context for what we are really like. Whatever the case may be, Dudu is cognizant of his act's wide popularity and continues to enrich himself on the backs of a marginalized group. It doesn't help either that Israelis have few iconic Mizrahi figures to idolize. And even when they do, as could be the case for Osnat Mark or Miri Regev, they're mocked relentlessly.

The reach of Ashkenormativity has also found its way into Israel's media institutions. One example involved Reina Abutbul, a ninety-two-year-old who immigrated from Morocco with her ten children over a decade ago. In 2020, in recognition for her incredible volunteer work, she became one of the few Mizrahi women ever to be named as one of the twelve people who light the torches at the national Independence Day celebration. Considering this list consists primarily of Ashkenazi Jews year after year, Abutbul's recognition was viewed as a big achievement. It comes as no surprise that this honor was handed down by Miri Regev herself, minister of cultural affairs at the time, who noted that she was trying to diversify the list by picking Abutbul and a few other Mizrahim.

In celebrating this crowning achievement, Keren Marciano, a senior news anchor for Channel 12, issued a public congratulatory sentiment to Abutbul on air. Marciano, who herself is from a Moroccan Jewish family, congratulated Abutbul with a few words in Judeo-Moroccan. The reaction from the Mizrahi community was something I'd never seen before, as dozens of people I knew, and many more online, were more ecstatic at Marciano's shout-out than Abutbul's honor.

The fact that a few words of Judeo-Moroccan uttered by a famous TV journalist lit up the internet tells me a lot about the Mizrahi place in Israeli society and demonstrates how Israelis are overdue for a national reckoning. In an interview afterward, Marciano said she was surprised by the reactions but acknowledged the large subset of the population who feel unseen and unheard.

When it comes to politics, both the perception and the reality of how Mizrahi Jews vote are light-years behind where they should be.

I've already mentioned how pervasive the perception is that Mizrahi Jews who vote for Right-wing candidates are seen as not voting in their own best interest. At the same time, there is a prevailing belief that when you speak about the Netanyahu voters, you're really talking about Mizrahim. Much as it was during Prime Minister Begin's time, Mizrahim who vote Likud are portrayed as barbaric. On the other hand, Likud-voting Ashkenazim are more likely to be taken seriously as considering nuance and weighing the options rationally.

Time and time again, elitist Ashkenazi journalists and news personalities go out of their way to identify Mizrahim who support Netanyahu and then turn them into a subject of mockery. Of course, this almost always backfires, as Mizrahi politicians use these incidents to gain sympathy by showing voters that they too understand what it's like to be the target of unspoken, often unconscious racism.

Regev, it seems, likes to double down on her under-class image by being deliberately loud and vulgar, resonating with voters who respect her unwillingness to play the Ashkenormative game. Regev's supporters can identify with what the Left-wing Ashkenazi newspaper *Haaretz* says about her, because they themselves are subject to similar insults in the streets and in the public sphere. It's not so different from the approach of former UK prime minister Boris Johnson, a bright man who does not fix his hair, speaks like a commoner, and is a caricature of every Brit's awkward alcoholic uncle. Needless to say, his voters loved him for that.

This trend follows Mizrahim wherever they go and seems to pop up even more frequently when they've proven their success. In 2007, Moroccan-born politician Amir Peretz, who was the first Mizrahi leader of the Labor Party, ascended to the post of minister of defense. Despite this incredible accomplishment, one of the things he's most known for is being the subject of a photo in which he is trying to look through a pair of binoculars with the lens caps on. That picture, which turned Peretz's gaffe into a punchline, won a photography award in Israel.

When Avi Gabbay, one of only a handful of successful Mizrahi businessmen, ran to lead the traditionally Ashkenazi-controlled Israeli Labor Party, he was quickly reminded of his place. Though he was elected in 2017, he'd eventually step down two years later after the Labor Party had its worst electoral showing in recent history. This was due in large part to the fact that he merely entertained an offer to join Prime

Minister Netanyahu's coalition during a meeting with him. Unfortunately, Gabbay is widely viewed as a failed politician despite accomplishing far more than those in his own party would give him credit for.

In contrast, Benny Gantz, an Ashkenazi politician who promised his voters that he'd never join a coalition with Netanyahu, ended up doing just that in 2020, and yet is still perceived as a serious Israeli politician. In fact, Gantz won eight seats (out of 120) in the March 2021 elections, giving his party the second-highest number of seats in the Israeli Left-wing bloc.

Another Mizrahi voice who has challenged Netanyahu from the Left is Orly Levy-Abekasis, who is one of twelve children of Moroccan-born former foreign affairs minister David Levy. In 2019, Levy-Abekasis formed her own party, called Gesher, to contest the April 2019 elections.

Although the party failed to win a single seat in that election, she returned to the Knesset following the September 2019 elections, in which Gesher formed a joint parliamentary list together with Gabbay's Labor Party. This contributed to the already sour taste of many Labor members who traditionally favored Ashkenazi leaders like themselves. In May 2020, Levy-Abekasis was appointed by Prime Minister Netanyahu to the newly created post of minister for community empowerment and advancement.

It is peculiar that despite all the rhetoric about how Labor is the party of fairness and inclusion, the Ashkenazi-dominated faction just can't seem to come to grips with a Mizrahi politician in power. At the same time, it's the leader of Likud, for all his flaws and foibles, who is creating opportunities for up-and-coming Mizrahi leaders.

Things really do trickle down into Israeli society: they see past the rhetoric and notice who promotes Mizrahim, and who doesn't.

I've seen this in my own life. My Mizrahi cousin recently told me that she has a colleague—a young, fair-skinned Ashkenazi woman—who resents the way in which she is favored by her boss for her professionalism. Later my cousin told me that her boss said something about how envious she was of my cousin's skin color. Her Ashkenazi colleague overheard this from the other room and walked in to say, "Oh come on! We are Ashkenazi ladies. Brown color doesn't, well, fit us." This reminds me, in a way, of *The Devil Wears Prada*, except tainted with colorism. With my cousin, she drew the ire of a coworker who believed she was receiving favorable treatment because of her darker skin color, while Anne Hathaway's character gets similarly positive treatment when she starts dressing nicer. With examples like these, it's important to note that while my cousin's boss's comment may seem like a harmless observation about ethnicity or skin color, they add up to a point where Mizrahim feel othered even when intentions are good.

While I do hear many stories like this secondhand, I have no question that the feeling is very real. Time and time again as I've navigated from early adulthood to my military service to seeking employment in the professional world, I've been made to feel "less than" for my Mizrahi background.

When I applied for what became one of my last jobs before I started my career as a writer and advocate for Mizrahi awareness, my prospective boss said something similar during my first interview. He asked me where my last name, Mazzig, came from. I told him it was from the Amazigh tribe in Tunisia. It's the truth, after all, a truth that took me years to come to terms with.

"You're Tunisian? That's very brave of you to say that," he said.

I told him that I am very proud of my heritage, to which he replied, "Proud? I wanted to say that I'll try not to hold it against you."

I have no doubt that he meant it in jest. I understand humor. But this was another pebble in a mountain that's been gradually growing higher and higher around me for years, and it's exhausting. I suppose my being Mizrahi wasn't actually "held against me," since I did get the job, but these kinds of jokes add up to something that isn't very funny. He didn't hold it against me, but he made a point of it. The subtext is obvious—that there are many cases where it *is* held against people. And if this had been such a case, I might not have been hired and, therefore, wouldn't have been able to earn a living, keeping me on the lower rungs of society. This idea, that my family background could keep me from getting a job, is a fear that Ashkenazim never have to worry about in Israel. In the Diaspora, many Jews know this feeling—and they rightly call it antisemitism.

This is the reality that so many Mizrahim still face in Israel—that is, if they can even get to interview for high-paying jobs at all. Though I didn't push back at the time—I was caught off guard and didn't want to risk not getting the job—I've vowed to do better since then. I believe my articles, my off-line and online activism, speaking engagements on campuses worldwide, and this book are evidence of that.

It is hard to describe how often each of us encounters this feeling, over so many years, to the point that many of us just accept it as the way of the world—an acceptance that is itself the intolerable, unstated goal of the Ashkenormative world around us: that we Mizrahim never forget our place.

On my thirtieth birthday, I rented a fairly nice venue to host a party for a group of my closest friends. In the process of planning the evening, the woman in charge of the establishment, who was Ashkenazi, asked me what type of drinks I wanted to serve to my guests. As I was in the beginning phases of embracing my ethnic heritage, I requested to serve

Arak. It just so happens that Arak is considered by many to be a drink most often consumed by Mizrahim (Dudu Faruk even has a song dedicated to his love of Arak). The woman looked at me in a way that made me feel like I was unhinged for even suggesting such a thing, and then she said, "That's not the type of place we are."

Matters got worse, from her perspective, when she learned that I had hired a Mizrahi drag queen to do a performance for my guests. Oh, the horror. It wasn't that she had anything against drag queens—she actually loved the idea. But then she learned the performer was Mizrahi, and her whole demeanor changed. For the rest of the evening, she seemed oddly fixated on the volume of our music. This too is a well-known code. Some might call it a micro-aggression, but boy, it feels macro to me.

Even those who provided great comfort to me when I was struggling with coming out as gay did not know how to address the Mizrahi aspect of my identity. Earlier, I told you about my IDF commander with whom I first shared my sexual orientation. Though his reaction to my being gay was an incredible relief, it wasn't quite the same when he discovered I was Mizrahi. He made a comment about how "we still accept you people." Again, he was joking, but it was enough for me never to bring it up again.

I was troubled. How could it be that coming out as gay turned out to be easier than coming out as Mizrahi? On the one hand, this could very well be a reflection of how far we have come in terms of LGBTQ equality and acceptance in Israel. In many countries, even popular travel destinations for Westerners, I would be subject to persecution for simply walking down the street holding my boyfriend's hand. But in Israel, as is the case in the US, Canada, and many other countries from Australia to even Mexico, thousands gather in the streets every summer for massive pride parades. Not to mention the embrace of the LGBTQ community by those in media, Hollywood, and academia. This is something to be celebrated, and I am grateful for such progress.

At the same time, it is also a reflection of how far we still have to go when it comes to Mizrahi acceptance. After all, when I get shouted down at universities and called a murderer by rage-filled students, they never disparage me because of whom I love. It's not just because I'm a progressive Israeli Zionist, but because I'm a person of color, a Mizrahi, and this above everything else drives them insane. By not fitting into their preconceptions of the enemy as a White-supremacist Jew, by not conforming to their narrative, I get deep under their skin.

The uncomfortable truth is that coming out as Mizrahi shouldn't require courage. Liberal societies don't give the same treatment to other minorities for being proud of their heritage, so why should Mizrahim endure such abuse (and, alternatively, neglect) for merely embracing our shared history and unique cultural traits? In a truly open and accepting society, this wouldn't even be a question.

I also deal with other classic stereotyping, including being stopped far more often at airport security. I don't know if it's my olive complexion or the strange last name that "won't be held against me," but whatever it is, I see that I am treated differently. On nearly every occasion I've traveled to the United States, I've been pulled aside and questioned at border control.

I experienced this further while living in Seattle for a short time in 2014, when a cop pulled me over on the highway and asked for my ID. When I handed him my Israeli passport, he replied, "I thought you were one of 'em al-Qaeders." I was relieved that he was fond of Israel, and it's possible he let me go because he thinks Israel is a White country. Still, being profiled because of my complexion left me feeling uneasy in a country I wasn't too familiar with.

Being a Jew of color, and particularly a Mizrahi, carries with it a set of connotations, criticisms, and assumptions, all perfectly designed to tamp down our voices and cast us aside. This occurs, first of all, within Jewish communities everywhere—we are marginalized in Israel and erased in the Diaspora.

When Donald Trump won the 2016 US presidential election, America's politicians, media, celebrities, and scholars were left dumbfounded. In the collective elite's fury to find any possible explanation as to how it could have happened, one rationale proved to be too enticing for the talking heads to pass up: it was White women's fault.

As Columbia University sociologist Musa al-Gharbi pointed out in a November 2020 article in the *Guardian*, the widely held perception then was that White women who voted for Donald Trump in 2016 were "uniquely motivated by racism—despite the fact that voters were choosing between two tickets comprised 100% of white people."[5]

As al-Gharbi writes, however, the exit polls from the 2020 election make that claim, retroactively, hard to sustain. For while White women did vote for Trump at higher rates in 2020 compared to 2016, so too did Black and Hispanic women, not to mention LGBTQ and Muslim Americans. Biden won not because minorities came out for him in force, but because "defections of *white men* overrode the preferences of this growing share of women and minorities."

This result reignited a debate that still seems to befuddle American commentators: why do members of minority communities *vote against* their own best interest?

Israel too has had a similar question asked after almost every election of my lifetime. Why, it is asked, do Mizrahim vote against their own best interest?

Ahead of the 2021 Knesset elections, the question was asked once again. Mizrahim—who again make up half the electorate—continued, by and large, to support Netanyahu despite incessant claims from the Left that he and his party were racist. Even when Mizrahi leadership emerged from the Left to challenge Netanyahu, it still wasn't enough to capture a significant portion of Mizrahi votes.

Those on the Right who chose to oppose Netanyahu don't seem to be able to garner much support from Mizrahim either. In 2021, MK (Member of Knesset) Gideon Sa'ar broke from Netanyahu's Likud to start the New Hope party. Sa'ar named MK Yifat Shasha-Biton, a child of Moroccan and Iraqi immigrants, as his number two, and half of the party's candidates were Mizrahim. Even though Shasha-Biton was the official who oversaw the Knesset's coronavirus committee, which was viewed by the Israeli public as critical to bringing Israel out of this pandemic, Sa'ar's party still only got six out of 120 Knesset seats.

In his 2012 article "Beyond the Garden and the Jungle: On the Social Limits of Human Rights Discourse in Israel," Nissim Mizrachi, former chair of the Department of Sociology and Anthropology at Tel Aviv University, offered several explanations for why Mizrahim vote the way they do.

"I think the most blatant phenomenon in world politics today is the resounding defeat of the liberal vision," Mizrachi said in an interview with Israeli newspaper *Haaretz*. "It's a double breakdown: one involving the government, in the sense of the left's inability to gain a political foothold among the masses; and more deeply, one involving an inability to imagine an order that accommodates opposition groups."[6]

Mizrachi gives little credence to many of the most popular rationales we often hear today about the Mizrahi vote. He avoids invoking pop psychology theories like false consciousness, herd instinct, battered wife syndrome, or Stockholm syndrome. On the contrary, he is saying: those suffering worst from blindness are the liberals who think that if they put Mizrahim at the top of a Left-wing party's electoral slate, then Mizrahi voters will vote for them en masse.

The problem is not the messenger, Mizrachi maintains in the same interview for *Haaretz*. "Rather, the liberal left must itself reexamine the message it's disseminating. To do that, however, it must display humility—a rare commodity among people who see themselves as the standard bearers of moral progressivism."

I've engaged in countless conversations like these. Nearly every time I speak with liberals about Mizrahi voting patterns, they struggle to come to terms with the fact that their *ideas* are seen as the problem, especially by the very people they want to help.

They often attribute the decisions of my community to false consciousness, which Mizrachi says is a kind of discourse that functions as an act of objectification. In other words, to say that Mizrahi Jews in Israel "vote against their best interests" because of a "false consciousness" strips us of our agency.

Mizrahim, he continues, don't necessarily see inequities as a form of injustice that must be fixed through structural or political change. On the contrary, he writes, Mizrahim generally "do not see themselves as suffering individuals getting a bad deal from the state. They are confident that the person at the top of the political pyramid is working for their collective good. Maybe it's not going well for him, but they don't suspect him of acting out of motives that are not to their benefit. He is coping with the problems, and the alternatives aren't necessarily better—just the opposite, in fact."[7]

In the 2021 elections, Netanyahu made a concerted effort to reach out to Arab-Israeli voters, as well. His efforts, it seems, garnered an additional two seats for Likud. This raised eyebrows in liberal circles in Israel. Not only were the Mizrahim voting against their own interests—now Arab Israelis were as well. *How stupid could they be?*

Examining how we got here requires that we dive a little deeper. Mizrahi Jews in Israel, alongside the Arab-Israeli population, are perceived as being primarily on the lower end of the socioeconomic hierarchy. Given the choice between voting for an elitist Ashkenazi on the Right, like Sa'ar, or an elitist Ashkenazi on the Left, the choice isn't clear-cut. This is because the political dynamic in Israel, as is the case in the United States, has much more to do with *class* than race. My father's experience with the Israeli Ashkenazi Left-wing elite in his younger years bears this out.

Since the days of Prime Minister Begin in 1977, the dominant view in Israel has been that the working class, made up mostly of marginalized Mizrahim, are the ones who brought Likud to power and continue to vote that way today. In 2021, I noticed a shift from the question of why Mizrahim vote for Likud to *who* are the Mizrahi voters. Are we indeed this lower-class, uneducated stereotype of Arab-cultured *arsim* and *frechot* who vote out of ignorance, while the Ashkenazi intellectual Left is trying to save the country?

In Israel, we have yet to fix or even seriously address these social issues, mainly because class issues surrounding Mizrahim are still taboo. The story of Israel's founding is depicted in the Jewish Diaspora as a legendary project of brave Jewish pioneers. However, we rarely talk about the fact that these very same people actively marginalized and oppressed Mizrahim. The sentiment is that voting for the Left-wing Mapai party, the forerunner of Labor, would mean supporting the very people that many Mizrahim hold accountable for historic injustices that have never been corrected or seriously addressed.

This is why trying to understand Israel in Western terms is a failed proposition from the outset. The notion of systemic racism, at least as it is manifested in America, cannot be symmetrically placed on top of Israel's society, because the majority of the population is made up of people of color. Our country never allowed slavery, nor do we live with the permanent stain of racism from generations past. While we have been influenced by Western ideas, it is not at the core of the country's identity—it's not our main story.

Israel also cannot be compared to Britain's classist system, as Mizrahi Jews can (and sometimes do) climb the socioeconomic ladder, while in the UK it is almost impossible for the working class to climb the social ladder. I believe that Israel falls somewhere in between these two social structures in the UK and US, with one important caveat: Israel is a country with a Jewish story, which upholds human rights with liberal and progressive ideas, but is not perfect and is constantly improving. While our political leaders, much like many of the citizens, have the capacity to be rude to one another, we are a moral people striving to improve the country we call home.

Regardless of what the screaming protesters may say, Israel does not fight wars with carpet bombing, and we do not engage in ethnic cleansing. The Israel Defense Forces, as the name indicates, is about defense, not aggression. We send our soldiers to a front line that is not thousands of miles away, but several hours by bus. We fight not for global democracy or oil profits, but for our lives and our safety.

The truth is that while Israel embodies cultural aspects seen in Europe, in the Middle East, and even in America, it has a distinctly Jewish heart and soul.

———◆◆◆———

In 2016, then education minister Naftali Bennett established the Biton Commission to infuse the Israeli education system with the Mizrahi story.

Announcing the launch, Bennett emphatically said, "We cannot raise a generation that knows only half of its legacy, and we cannot educate youth to 'love thy neighbor as thyself' when youth do not know their 'neighbor' that constitutes at least half of their class."

The committee was named for Erez Biton, the first poet of Mizrahi heritage to win the Israel Prize in Literature and Poetry (2015) and Bennett's choice to lead the group. Biton, who has been blind since childhood, was born in Algeria, and his well-known works include 1976's *Mincha Marokait* (*A Moroccan Gift*) and 1979's *Sefer Hanana* (*The Book of Mint*).

"Eastern Jewry should not be ashamed; Zionism was ingrained in her from the belly and through birth. Now we want our contribution to also be evident in the educational curriculum, that also our contribution to Zionism will be heard and taught,"[8] Biton said.

While I was thrilled by the creation of the commission, some voices in Israel were less enthused. Arie Rutenberg, the founder of one of Israel's biggest PR firms, a branch of the global advertising agency McCann Erickson, posted the following on Facebook (translated from Hebrew):

> Do not take it too much to heart. The Mizrahim are inferior to the Westerners...Every Jewish community brought with them their culture...The *yekke* [i.e., German Jews] are thorough, serious, precise, educated, like the Germans, and Miri Regev is the reflection of the Moroccan culture as a whole. Don't take it too hard but the east is far behind the west, and with it so were the Mizrahi Jews...The question is how do we want to raise our children? With an advanced European culture or a retarded Mizrahi culture? The Biton Commission is taking us backwards.[9]

In 2018, award-winning Israeli director Maor Zaguri penned a response to Rutenberg's sentiments, in a piece that takes aim not at Ashkenazi Jews as a whole, but at any Jews who hold racist beliefs. He also took a swing at the many Israelis, primarily on the Left, who have started to suggest that it is time to leave Israel because the country has changed to a point where they feel like it no longer resembles a democracy. As Zaguri put it:

They say that they are afraid to raise their children in this country. Who do you think you are anyway? You think that we won't make it without you? You and your friends, the racist White Panthers, are welcome to leave Israel. Understand that Israel is not going anywhere. Israel is doing very well and without you we will do even better. After the last of these racists leave, we will be able to live together; Ashkenazim and Mizrahim will live side by side in peace. Maybe we will also have peace with our neighbors. You couldn't even get along with us Jews from Arab lands, so how would you ever get along with Arab-Muslims?[10]

Zaguri perfectly articulated the problem. This is not a story of Mizrahim versus Ashkenazim. It is a tale of a small yet powerful group of elitists who think that just because they're of European descent, they are superior. Their claim of universal justice hides a bitter parochialism: this group shows preference to Eurocentric ideas while disregarding Mizrahi culture, which they dismiss as inferior and backward.

———◆———

A lot of underrepresented groups express a shared senti-ment that they want fair treatment and equal representation. And being who I am, what I believe in, and what I've fought for, I acknowledge that each of these identities, from African

Americans to LGBTQ to indigenous peoples, make valid points that must be addressed in order for all of us to live up to the democratic ideals of tolerance and equality.

But that is not what this book is about.

I am Mizrahi, a proud member of a group that has not only been marginalized wherever we've called home, but who have been deceived and used as pawns in very specific ways. The result of which is that even within the most progressive, intersectional spaces, our story is rarely heard. Even within the Diaspora Jewish community itself, most people don't even know that close to a million Jews from Arab and Muslim countries fled centuries-long persecution only to be pushed to the back of the bus in their ancestral homeland and rendered invisible around the world.

In the last few years, important strides have been made to raise the voices of people of color in both the United States and Europe. We have seen large corporations reexamine their own policies as they relate to diversity and inclusion. The stories of marginalized people are being told more and more in film and media. For Mizrahim, however, little has changed. The depiction of Jews in Hollywood films and television series tends to be still almost exclusively Ashkenazi. Even the few Israelis who make it in Hollywood are almost all Ashkenazi.

The advancement of voiceless minorities has been an amazing achievement of the progressive movement. In that vein, it is now time for these same groups to open doors to the Mizrahi people. Because the fact is that to truly solve the issues I've presented in this book, we need to claim our own voice. I can give speech after speech after speech, but this will only create progress at an incremental rate compared to what could occur if Mizrahim saw themselves as who they truly are: a unique identity with a specific culture and traditions and a shared experience, centuries in the making, that unites them through challenges and victories alike.

You might ask: *Well, Hen, how much is enough?* This is always asked of minorities looking for a voice, with the assumption being that because we don't quantify our demands, we will never stop asking for more. After all, I did mention that Mizrahim have served in the Knesset and as government ministers in Israel, while others have climbed to senior positions in major media organizations and won coveted national prizes. But the dramatic underrepresentation continues, and these examples feel more like tokens than recognition.

So at this stage, in Israel at least, the only reasonable answer is that *more is better.* We need to highlight achievements in Mizrahi music to counter the negative perception presented by Dudu Faruk and the like. We need more Mizrahi politicians to show that we are not all either ardent Right-wingers or Left-wing self-deniers. We need more Mizrahi teachers, cultural leaders, and medical professionals to demonstrate that we have a lot to offer the world, and we must shatter the pervasive notion that there is a ceiling to our capacities. In turn, this will propel young Mizrahi kids to think and dream big, and thrust many of them into influential roles within society.

In the Diaspora, and especially in North America where more than 90 percent of Jews are Ashkenazi, the task is somewhat different. Our first step here is educational: to demand an end to the erasure of our heritage. To bind together the extremely diverse community of Jews of color—from African American and Latino Jews to Persian, Syrian, and Moroccan Jews—all under a single identity, without taking away from the more specific identities of each group. And we must—*must*—retell the story of Israel, not just as the "State of the Jews," but as the state of the Jews of color. Our biggest problem is not with those who hate Israel—antisemitism is, after all, a fixture of human history, which we must fight tooth and nail but never be surprised at.

Rather, our problem is with those, like the pro-Israel organization I worked for in Seattle, who claim to love Israel but understand almost nothing about it because they are blind to this central truth: that Mizrahim today constitute the biggest Jewish community in Israel.

And we have to internalize, before everything else, that the burden is on us to create our own voice. Until Jews of color in America understand that they are not just a small minority of American Jews, but also represent *millions* of voiceless Jews around the world—until they take this immense burden upon themselves—they won't be able to build the institutions, the educational messages, the publications, and the coherent philanthropic and professional networks that giving ourselves a voice will require.

Nobody will hand it to us on a platter. If we want to be heard, we will have to get much, much louder.

However, in order to do this, we must fully acknowledge the scope and presence of Ashkenormativity, and how it works to divide Jews of color into disconnected cantons. While I vehemently defend the Jewish people against antisemitism, support the democratic ideals on which Israel was founded, take pride in my IDF service, and am grateful that my family and so many Mizrahim found refuge here, I also know that my people and my country have propped up a Eurocentric narrative at the expense of Jews of color. It's no wonder that irate university students accuse me of being a "racist White enabler of genocide against brown people" for supporting Israel, when Israel and the pro-Israel community continue to sell an image of the country as essentially European and White.

We must also strip down the divisiveness that comes with the ongoing debate about Mizrahi Jews. There can be absolutely no solution to the struggles of Mizrahim if the very idea of acknowledging our unique heritage within the context of our shared story is somehow deemed toxic or threatening. We cannot have the "but we're all Jews" discussion while Jewish scholars claim that our identity is Israeli government propaganda, when non-Jewish commentators say we're just Arabs. We can't be "all Jews" until all of us *feel* that we're all Jews, that we are recognized and accepted in every Jewish space, and that Ashkenazi Jews go out of their way to defend Mizrahi identity against its erasure, instead of facilitating it. I would never ask anyone to abandon their culture or identity in order to feel more equal, and the same thing should never be asked of me or any other Mizrahi.

Not all Jews are White. Even if you accept that a great many Jews in the Diaspora have benefited from White privilege, this is not the case for Jews of color—including and especially Mizrahim. If anything, we are targeted from more directions. We face antisemitism, we face claims of privilege when we have none, we face rejection and erasure from within our own community merely because of our skin color, heritage, and culture. And our inconvenient identity is simply denied, *defined out of existence*, by woke spokespeople like Linda Sarsour and Marc Lamont Hill.

Mizrahim aren't really demanding a whole lot. We want the world to know who we are, and we want our fellow Jews to recognize us as equals. We can recognize that while Ashkenormativity can harm the Jewish community, we must also be united as a people. I believe that recognizing this reality will empower our community in extraordinary ways.

5.

THE MIZRAHI MANIFESTO

Every year, a group of a few dozen, mostly older Jews comes together in the early summer to hold a ceremony in the Tel Aviv suburb of Or Yehuda, not far from the airport.

At this ceremony, an elderly Jew will get up to the microphone and speak. A heavy Iraqi accent will make it difficult to understand what he or she is saying. Like clockwork, the speakers will start tearing up as they share the horrors they endured, perhaps when they were just teenagers. In the burning sun of the summer in Or Yehuda, they will read a prayer for those who did not survive, conclude the ceremony, and walk back to their homes.

On the walls of the small Babylonian Jewry Heritage Center, where this ceremony takes place, there's one testimony from 1941. It is old, and a few of the letters are missing. It reads:

The door suddenly broke open.

My mother stood by the door, and I stood behind her...

Our neighbors ente[re]d, and so did other Arabs...

My mother said to them (in Arabic):

"The house and everything in it is yours. Just don't hurt us."

They started taking out objects one after the other.

In the midst of the looting, a policeman in uniform entered...

He stood there and cursed our religion and Palestine (in Arabic).

Mother kept begging...

He shot her in the head, and she fell.

I fled and stood behind the policeman.

My olde[r] sister ran towards her: "Mother, mother!"

A rioter was standing on the roof; he took hold of my younger brother

and wanted to slaughter him...

My (other) sister begged: "Child, child, why are you killing him?"

My cousin wanted to go upstairs.

The rioter opened her belly, and everything fell out.[1]

The reason this ceremony—unlike many of the other traditions for victims of antisemitic violence—does not get any serious recognition, even in Israel, is that it memorializes a story of the invisible: the Mizrahi Jewish community.

This ceremony commemorates the Farhud in 1941, as well as the public hangings of Jews in Iraq in the 1960s and '70s.

Not one member of the Knesset or government minister has ever found the time to join them.

For the ceremony in 2020, the group invited me to speak. When they introduced me, they referred to me as a grandchild of a survivor. "Grandchild of a survivor" is a title many of my friends in Israel have—but all of them are Ashkenazi Jews whose grandparents survived the Holocaust. I've never been included in that group. It doesn't matter that my great-grandparents too survived the Nazis. The Vichy regime sent my Tunisian father's grandparents to a forced labor camp during the Holocaust. They were due to be sent to death camps in Europe. My Iraqi grandparents also were victimized by the Third Reich; they survived the Farhud, which Nazi supporters in Baghdad incited at the same time the Nazis were murdering Europe's Jews.

But the truth is that while I know the history of pain my Ashkenazi friends' grandparents endured, they don't know mine. While I know the names of many individual death camps in Nazi-era Europe, many of my friends, especially in the United States, have never heard of the Farhud. It is not taught in American Hebrew schools. It rarely appears in textbooks. The Mizrahi victims of the Holocaust have been erased twice—once from the earth and then from our collective memory.

It breaks my heart. And if you are sensitive to the suffering of Jews of the period, it should break yours as well.

I cannot believe there is an intentional agenda behind erasing the Mizrahi Jewish community's history from international academia and public discourse. Our exclusion does not feel deliberate on most days. But when we point out our absence from the conversation, and members of our community shame us as "divisive," it's hard not to see this erasure as an act of malice. The Mizrahi community is not looking to divide the world's Jewry. We just want to be included in the greater narrative of our tribe. We want our faces, histories, and traditions to be seen as an integral part of the Jewish experience, rather than an alien or exotic permutation.

I remember the first time I wrote about the exclusion of Mizrahim from Holocaust remembrance for a Jewish American online publication a few years ago. My intention was absolutely not to undermine anyone else's intergenerational trauma, but to broaden the discussion. I want to be acknowledged as the grandson of a survivor, and not just by an isolated group of Iraqi Jews.

The responses to my speaking on this issue were disturbing and highlight how much resistance Mizrahi Jews face when seeking any recognition. We struggle to have our ancestry written into the Jewish story, but we are dealing with a culture where many refuse to even acknowledge our absence.

For telling the same story I used to open this chapter, I was accused of harming the memory of the Holocaust. Numerous Ashkenazi Jews reminded me their kin were the "primary victims" of the atrocities, and that my efforts to shine a light on my grandparents' victimization somehow minimized that of their own grandparents.

Here's the thing: I do not believe that my light dilutes your light. I do not believe that memory is a pool that can accommodate only so many swimmers.

It's not lost on me that this trend of dismissing Mizrahi history as some kind of attack on the mainstream Ashkenazi narrative mirrors the current discussion of race in America. We see that debate everywhere; it's amplified in the charged conversation on where the trials of African Americans and the horrors of slavery belong in education. I've closely followed the intense backlash to the 1619 Project and how some institutions have even banned it from being taught in schools.

Now, whether or not you believe Nikole Hannah-Jones's narrative of America is historically accurate or academically valid, there can be no doubt that the history of minorities in the West (including Jews) has been underrepresented in every aspect of American culture. I reject the erasure of well-known figures or the replacement of majority history with that of minorities, as we saw when the San Francisco Board of Education voted, in January 2021, to remove the names of Abraham Lincoln, Thomas Jefferson, and others from schools. (They have since reversed that decision.) However, I do identify with the people of color in America who accuse their White counterparts of having a certain "fragility" when discussing disparities in modern society.

I would never accuse Ashkenazi Jews of White fragility, because even white-skinned Ashkenazi Jews have never been entirely accepted into European or American Whiteness. However, some have expressed to me discomfort and defensiveness when confronted with the glaring inequalities in our community.

I understand that in living memory, Nazis brutally murdered six million Jews. If this genocide were not enough, antisemites worldwide actively erase, deny, and denigrate that history of violence and death. The trauma that Ashkenazi Jews carry, combined with the efforts to erase them, makes every conversation about this history triggering and painful. It doesn't help that many who claim to be progressive or proponents of communities like mine actively participate in whitewashing the realities of antisemitism or push hateful conspiracies that Jews are uniquely racist or behind oppression in America.

However, when bigots attack the memory of the Holocaust, it affects all Jews, and not just those whose families endured it. Mizrahim have no intention to contribute to the culture of chipping away at Shoah remembrance. We just want to be reasonably integrated into the practice.

The irony is that amplifying Mizrahi history can actually be a source of unity, not division, in the American Jewish community. I identify so strongly with my friends whose grandparents survived the Holocaust in Eastern Europe. One of my closest friends is an American Ashkenazi Jew whose grandmother survived Auschwitz. Her father was born in a displaced persons camp in Germany.

In our friendship, she doesn't interpret my talking about my family history as somehow minimizing hers. So we speak often about the tortuous trials of our bloodlines. This openness has given us a shared language, a platform to relate. I can discuss with her the feeling of displacement, our identification with refugees, and the existential fear of the world turning a blind eye as our communities bleed out. Her father lived in makeshift tents, just as my mother did. We are children of kindred traumas.

I believe that Jews as a whole are children of similar traumas, and bringing attention to an underrepresented faction of our tribe doesn't undermine Ashkenazi history—or any other oppressed person's history—but fundamentally creates space for it to be better understood and heard. The inclusion of Mizrahi Jews should be a foundation for more empathy, and we should never reject more compassion.

But by silencing the conversation about Mizrahim, the message young Mizrahi Jews receive is that our story doesn't matter.

In early 2020, I posted a picture online (because if you know me, you know I post everything online). It had me with two of my friends at a Yemenite restaurant in south Tel Aviv. I captioned it: "Teaching my Ashkenazi friends what Mizrahi food is all about...Visit Salouf & Sons next time you're in Tel Aviv and get the Kubana, I promise you won't regret it!"

I thought it was a great opportunity to support an excellent restaurant. Many people loved the shout-out, but one comment stood out to me. It came from a rabbi of Ashkenazi descent. Before he was ordained, he was a successful journalist covering Arab issues in Israel. Politically, he was very Left-wing and a staunch supporter of anti-Israel causes.

"I had no idea you were Yemenite," he commented.

I am not—it is apparent to anyone who knows my work, particularly this rabbi, who is aware that my family is from Iraq and Tunisia. So the comment felt pointed. I chose not to respond, but one of my followers offered a snarky rebuttal: "I wonder how people can write but can't read!"

"I actually read Arabic in addition to English," the rabbi fired back. "Does that make me Mizrahi, or do I need to have the Kubana gene?"

Now, Kubana is a traditional Yemenite Jewish bread that is popular in Israel among many, mostly disadvantaged, Mizrahim. Since it's delicious and doesn't have many ingredients, it's cheap to make and popular among many Mizrahim, not only Yemenites.

In a way, it has turned into the Mizrahi version of a challah, as it is often made on Friday night for Shabbat dinner. From this dish has come a slur, "kubana," a derogatory reference to the customs of Mizrahi Jews in Israeli culture. It's a way of mocking us as somehow barbaric and undeveloped. Like us, Kubana has Middle Eastern roots, so it is looked down upon in comparison to Western foods.

What this rabbi had just said was comparable to telling a Black American, "Does that make me Black, or do I need to have the fried chicken gene?"

People often claim to me that, despite all the evidence to the contrary, Mizrahi Jews do not experience racism from other Jews. This is one example of this prejudice, coming from a well-respected rabbi.

"Kubana gene?" I replied.

"In other words, what makes you closer to Yemenites than the Ashkenazi friends sitting at the table?" he replied, voicing the reason he had appeared in my comments section in the first place: He objected to the concept of Mizrahi being a communal identity that Jews who lived in Muslim lands shared. But he was happy to use the term *Ashkenazi*, which unifies Jews from across most of Europe as a shared ethnicity. Why did he recognize Ashkenazi and not, by the same standards, Russian or Polish or Ukrainian?

"I don't refer to other Mizrahi Jews as having the 'Kubana gene,' that's first," I wrote, because anyone with our culture, history, and experience of discrimination would fully understand the harm caused by that term.

I was trying to keep my cool after reading his comments, but struggled to even formulate a sentence through the keys. No one likes hearing a slur. But what was even more disturbing was having someone object to the very idea of a shared Mizrahi experience while validating that of his Ashkenazi community in the same sentence. Deep down, I knew that there was nothing I could say to win his respect. I was dealing with someone who believed he understood my family's culture and history better than I did.

He didn't stop. "Yemenites and, say, Iraqis, pray differently, follow different rabbinic authorities, and come from vastly different cultures. They share (different dialects of) Arabic. Bottom line: I don't buy the Mizrahi-Ashkenazi dichotomy," he concluded.

While I don't dispute his specific facts, it is bizarre to argue that there has never been a Mizrahi-Ashkenazi dichotomy. There are, of course, many cultural differences within the Mizrahi community, as there are in the Jewish community at large. No one questions if the shared identity of Ashkenazi

Jews is valid, even though the cultures of a Jew with roots in Berlin and another who comes from a shtetl in Ukraine are vastly different. Even American Jews have different accents, cuisines, and traditions.

These realities exist outside of the Jewish identity as well. For example, would this rabbi argue with a Yemenite Muslim for calling himself Arab even though he has a different national origin than an Iraqi one? Aren't Yemen and Iraq just as different culturally, regardless of religion? So why are Arab-Muslims of the region allowed an undisputed shared heritage but Jews denied one?

We can even go outside the Middle East to unpack this. According to the 2018 Indian census, more than 19,500 languages are spoken in the country as mother tongues. Formally, the country has twenty-two recognized languages. However, it doesn't matter if you speak Bengali or Urdu, all Indians are incontestably Indian.

What we culturally have in common always lives alongside, and may even override, our differences. Mizrahi Jews share an experience of mass expulsion, marginalization, food, music, and Judeo-Arabic heritage (regardless of which dialectic we use). Deep down, this rabbi knew this, because he knew that the slur "kubana" could be weaponized against me. We are all fighting against the same self-aggrandizing ignorance. So, in some ways, this rabbi is correct—to be Mizrahi, you do need the "Kubana gene," or at least to recoil at the phrase.

Nor is this experience limited to Israel. Similar slurs are thrown at Mizrahi Jews in the Diaspora as well. The town of Great Neck, New York, experienced an influx of Persian Jews fleeing post-revolution Iran in the 1980s, and many still live there today. But if you look up "Great Neck" at the Urban Dictionary website, you'll find a litany of contempt for Persian Jews. Here are some examples:

Great Neckers are cheap, whining, pushy people who buy everything on sale then check the receipt... as if auditing a tax return; on which they themselves cheated.

The Mecca for Iranian exiles... but in reality exemplify some of the worst ethnic stereotypes along with their older white brethren holdouts who haven't yet left for Florida. Great Neck is full of people who can be seen every morning, except Saturdays, finger mining for the morning catch while making illegal U-turns and talking on their cell phones.

Great Neck is well known for its top-ranking school districts and abundance of wealth. Unfortunately, many of the Iranian-American residents are pretentious and rude...While the town itself is very safe and the school districts are great, the horrible quality of people that inhabit the town make it almost unbearable for decent people to live in.

Great Neck is a town that Persians have, in the last 20 years, completely invaded. Instead being inhabited by normal, American Jews, Great Neck is now the home of thousands of Persians who feel the need to NEVER shave the bushes of hair they and their moms have had since birth. Every Persian in Great Neck also has a dying sensation to marry their own cousins. Each slutty girl in Great Neck, whether she's a normal Jew or a Persian, feels the need to flaunt what they don't have in Juicy outfits and $14,000 handbags. Where do Persians get this kind of money? Well, they claim to each "sell rugs". However, WHERE DO THEY GET THE MONEY TO BUY 16,000,000 DOLLAR HOMES is still a question left unanswered.

Great Neck is ... the worst town in the world. It is overpopulated by Persian whores that **** their cousins.

I am not Persian. But my family has been confronted with many of these same stereotypes. All Mizrahi Jews have. We are "cheap," "pushy," "hairy," and "rude." We are "exiles" and have been accused of making our neighborhoods "unbearable for decent people" by moving in. Most of all, we are not "normal Jews."

You do not have to speak Hebrew or know about Kubana to be told you have the "Kubana gene."

But I would rather focus on the food. In many Israeli restaurants, you will encounter something known as Mizrahi food. You can feast upon Yemenite *jahnun*, Iraqi *sabich*, Moroccan pickled vegetables, Egyptian falafel, and, of course, hummus, which the entire Middle East claims to have developed. The fact is that our positive culture, not just our oppression, has been exchanged, integrated, and, as a consequence, unified.

I believe that you can only add identities, not lose them, like delicacies to your menu. Being Mizrahi does not make me less Iraqi or Amazigh. It is an added layer, a resource for more connection and joy. I believe that there is no finite number of identities any person can hold. I can be Mizrahi and Iraqi, and Amazigh and Israeli and Jewish and gay and a brother and loud and a *RuPaul's Drag Race* aficionado. That is the beauty of my humanity and individuality. I am allowed to be limitless.

The world isn't high school, and life isn't a workweek; I have time to be a member of as many clubs as I like. Community and identity are infinite resources, and you are allowed to adopt as many as you'd want.

I advocate for a shared Mizrahi identity because Jews of the Middle East and North Africa experienced similar traumas and formative experiences. We must come together to strengthen and enrich ourselves—just as all Jews come together to fight antisemitism, preserve our history, and enjoy each other's company.

I am arguing to bring our community together, not to erase either our unique national heritage or our broader Jewish heritage. If your family came from Yemen or Iraq, each culture is special, beautiful, and should be celebrated. But why not bring many national identities under the Mizrahi umbrella, where we will celebrate all of them? Then we will bring them under the Jewish umbrella where Sephardi Jews from Panama and Ashkenazi Jews from Russia will learn about us.

In simpler terms, I am calling for unity through the recognition of our diversity. Unity is not uniformity.

In 2016, California became one of the first states in America to require its public schools to teach courses in ethnic studies. The initiative aimed at reimagining how students understand and ultimately fight against racism by focusing on the stories and contributions of historically marginalized groups—a marked break from the traditional curriculum. And while fervently backed by the state's predominantly progressive legislature, the first draft of the model curriculum, released in 2019, met immediate criticism, and not just from the Right.

A *Los Angeles Times* editorial called efforts to teach ethnic studies "critical" while also criticizing the initial proposal as "jargon-filled and all-too-PC."[2] A *New York Times* article several days later suggested that the draft curriculum presented a "dilemma" regarding "whose stories to tell,"[3] and raised questions about the intentions behind it as well as the impact such lessons would have on young people.

As much as I lament the current state of legacy media, with its partisan bias, whataboutism, and false balance, I found myself agreeing with both the praise and the criticism. The initial language was indeed jargony. It asked students, for example, to "critique empire and its relationship to White supremacy, racism, patriarchy, cis-heteropatriarchy, capitalism, ableism, anthropocentrism and other forms of power and oppression at the intersections of our society." It wasn't teaching the history of peoples, but rather that of "isms," which, in my mind, is not the foundation for greater compassion and understanding, as ethnic studies should be.

Such lofty activist vocabulary, moreover, left a lot open to interpretation. I know this because eerily similar language has become standard rhetoric for the very people who violently protest against me simply because I support my own country, using incendiary labels like "White majority," "White nationalist," or "White supremacist." (The emptiness of these statements is obvious when you consider that White nationalists are often explicitly anti-Israel and that I am often accused by *them* of being anti-White because I advocate for better representation of ethnic minorities in the Jewish community and beyond.)

So I shouldn't have been as shocked as I was to discover the most severe blind spot of this widely panned draft curriculum: Jews.

The story of what happened in California contains within it a microcosm of the challenges facing Jews, and especially Mizrahi Jews, in our current cultural moment, and it's worth taking a good look at what happened.

The backlash from Jewish groups to the draft was intense. A curriculum meant to oppose oppression and give voice to minorities had somehow failed to include *any* mention of antisemitism. This was pretty troubling in itself—Jews are the single most targeted religious group and the third most targeted ethnic group for hate crimes in America, despite being barely 2 percent of the population. Of course, the curriculum placed heavy emphasis on the Israeli-Palestinian conflict—but only from the Palestinian side, erasing Jewish indigeneity in the Middle East and taking an overtly political stance in endorsing boycotts of Israel.

Throughout this book, I have repeatedly expressed my objections to how Jews of color are portrayed and treated in Jewish society and culture, emphasizing our plight in Israel. However, I reject the notion that an effective ethnic studies curriculum requires that we teach students that white-skinned Jews are simply White people who face no oppression. Jews are just as susceptible to hate and bigotry in the form of antisemitism, even if they are not targeted because of their skin color. And while it's true that people can still be prejudiced and uphold racist systems even if they experience other forms of hate, such as antisemitism, it is precisely this

THE WRONG KIND OF JEW

kind of complexity that educational systems should embrace if they are to give students a true sense of humanity.

If the curriculum ignored the unique experience of Jews as an ethnic minority facing antisemitism, the experience of Middle Eastern Jews—and in fact, all Middle Eastern minorities, including Copts, Yazidis, Baha'is, and any other non-Muslims who have suffered for centuries under brutal oppression at the hands of Arab and Muslim regimes—was utterly erased. This subject is not an obscure technical matter for California either. Tens of thousands of Mizrahi kids will be forced to study the curriculum in California's schools and be affected by its cultural assumptions. As the Mizrahi educational group JIMENA pointed out in its official response:

> While the Middle East and North Africa is one of the most ethnically and religiously diverse regions in the world, within the model curriculum the term "Arab" is never defined leaving educators and readers to easily conflate "Arabs," "Muslims," and "Middle Easterners."... The Arab Studies Course['s] erasure of Jewish and minority Middle Eastern perspectives perpetuates a legacy of oppression and cultural genocide of non-Muslim Middle Eastern groups who fled persecution to find sanctuary in the United States.[4]

Indeed, JIMENA, which estimates that the state of California is home to some 236,000 Jews of Middle Eastern and North African descent, has been one of the only Jewish groups that have understood the nature of the problem. In a conversation I had with its executive director Sarah Levin, she said the organization spent most of the two-year battle in California advocating for the inclusion of Jews at all and fighting against the antisemitism found in the original curriculum. Even when Mizrahi Jews had the opportunity to center ourselves and our history, JIMENA chose to fight for *all* Jews and not just for a single subgroup. Without JIMENA's efforts, there would have been no inclusion of an antisemitism definition in the ethnic studies curriculum. But Jews of the Middle East were able to demand it.

This dynamic is the basis of much of my pro-Israel and Jewish advocacy. The contemporary Western conversation on oppression is highly racialized and often not complex. Jewish identity and Israel, however, are incredibly complex.

For the past decade or so, I have been able to use my Iraqi and Amazigh heritage to open the doors for Jews in progressive spaces. By driving home the reality that Jews like me exist, I've been able to begin a dialogue with numerous activists who are fixated on fighting only racism or have failed to include ending antisemitism as an action item. Since Jews of color experience antisemitism, it is an intersectional issue that antiracists need to address.

Do I think social justice advocates should, as a rule, combat antisemitism in general? Absolutely, and it is a complete shame how Jews of all backgrounds have been systematically excluded from numerous justice movements. However, my goal is to make all Jews safer in every space. If I can pave inroads in the progressive community toward understanding antisemitism and protecting Jews through my specific Mizrahi story, it is my responsibility to do so.

It's crucial that Mizrahi Jews—and Jews who don't fit neatly into more recognized marginalized groups—remember that amplifying our voices is an opportunity for greater inclusion. That's what JIMENA did when it came to the California ethnic studies curriculum—they not only sought recognition of our history and humanity but also strove to educate children about the prejudice that threatens all Jews.

When we Mizrahi Jews tell our stories, it helps all Jews become included in social justice movements.

None of this is meant to suggest that I object to teaching ethnic studies in schools—on the contrary. And thankfully, the controversy brought about some significant revisions to the curriculum, which today includes robust sections on both antisemitism and Mizrahi Jews.

That's great, you may say. There was a process of public discussion, an outcry, and a correction. The system worked, right?

But that's not what really happened.

The harshest critics of including Mizrahi Jews—and antisemitism in the ethnic studies curriculum—were not just the antisemites. JIMENA also experienced brutal backlash from Right-wing Ashkenazi Jews.

One Jewish critic was Emily Benedek, who penned a widely read January 2021 piece in *Tablet* titled "California Is Cleansing Jews from History." In her article, which retold the story of the controversy, she also took a swing at the entire concept of ethnic studies and critical race theory, which argues that race is a social construct that affects communities of color from all walks of life.

Benedek's forceful attack on the curriculum was undermined, however, by a few glaring missteps that made me question her intellectual honesty. She referenced, for example, antisemitic material from a previous draft that JIMENA had successfully lobbied to remove. She also claimed that she failed to acknowledge that the revised draft cites surging rates of hate crimes against Jews and how we are the most common victims of religious-based hate crimes in Southern California. She wrote:

> Capitalism was classified as a form of "power and oppression," and although "classism, homophobia, Islamophobia, and transphobia" were also listed as forms of oppression, anti-Semitism was not. Jewish Americans were not even mentioned as a minority group.

In this, Benedek failed to acknowledge that the new version had an entire lesson on Jews, including passages from noted opponents of antisemitism like Ruth Wisse, Julius Lester, and Rabbi Angela Buchdahl, or that it recognized that all Jews are indigenous to the Middle East. In fact, Benedek even claimed an article that was not in the curriculum was proof that ethnic studies are inherently corrupt, but the article was just in the same book as another passage referenced.

The most disturbing part of this article was that Benedek claimed that the abandoned draft included this quote on pre-war Zionism: "The Jews have filled the air with their cries and lamentations in an effort to raise funds and American Jews, as is well known, are the richest in the world." If this quote were actually included, I would be alarmed. However, these words were never in any draft of the curriculum or its readings.

When pressed on this, Benedek said it was in line 11180 of the curriculum's Appendix A. There, Ameen Rihani's essay "Deserts of Fact and Fancy" is cited. But this quote wasn't there either. It turns out this language wasn't in the curriculum, as Benedek had claimed, nor in the essay it recommended. This antisemitic quote was from a different, not-cited article that was printed in the same collection as "Deserts of Fact and Fancy." Not only was this statement never included in any draft of the curriculum, but it was thirty pages away in a separate publication from a reading it recommended.

When confronted with these errors, Benedek added an author's note five days after the essay was published. The writer explained why she elected not to mention or speak to the pro-Israel and Jewish organizations who worked for almost two years to include Jews in the curriculum: "The reason I felt no need to praise these tweaks is that they are peripheral to the problem."

But perhaps the most jarring element of Benedek's presentation appeared only after I confronted her on Twitter about the article. Her response was, it seemed, full of discomfort, particularly toward the inclusion of Mizrahi Jews in the curriculum. She tweeted that Jewish groups created the unit on Mizrahim only so Mizrahim "could argue they were [people of color]."[5] She then characterized the revised curriculum on Jewish history as being laden with "inter-tribal jealousies."

This was distressing. It was a huge win that California students would be taught about Mizrahi Jews. It was a landmark moment of recognition for my people. We have so little representation even within Jewish spaces. I often encounter people, both Jewish and not, who have never heard the term *Mizrahi* or that Jews have lived in the Middle East in recent history. I was appalled that Benedek, a well-decorated writer, particularly in Jewish publications, saw no merit in teaching children about Mizrahi heritage.

The subtext of her words—and, in retrospect, an underlying message of her article—was that the Mizrahi experience is "peripheral" to Jewish culture, and certainly is not worthy of study on its own. Even if we introduce education on antisemitism that benefits all Jews, it is somehow undermined by having specific recognition of Jews of the Middle East and North Africa.

No less offensive was her reference to "inter-tribal jealousies." There is always something unnerving about hearing someone refer to the calling out of discrimination and under-representation as a form of jealousy—but especially when it comes from someone who is doing the exact same thing on behalf of Jews as a whole. This kind of rhetoric reduces real inequalities into a petty game, and also seems tinged with prejudice: one can assume that Mizrahi Jews are "jealous" of the Ashkenazi majority only if one thinks we have less or, even worse, *are* less. And the use of a psychological explanation like jealousy is all too reminiscent of how Israeli Ashkenazim describe Mizrahi voting patterns as a "false consciousness"—it refuses to take us seriously, robbing us of our agency.

JIMENA worked hand in hand with Ashkenazi-dominated organizations to bring about major revisions to the draft curriculum, including specific mention of the Mizrahi experience. And yet Benedek took the opportunity of her author's note to lash out against the Mizrahi inclusion, and against my own criticisms. "It has been troubling, to say the least," she writes, "to watch some Jewish advocates use a fight with the state to balkanize the community into subgroups..."[6]

The Jewish community already exists in subgroups, and in fact always has, ever since the Israelites marched out of Egypt in their twelve tribes. There are Russian Jews, German Jews, American Jews, Iranian Jews, Ethiopian Jews. No one takes issue with teaching about these unique identities, so why is anyone offended by sharing the collective stories of Jews of the Middle East? Especially when sharing our history empowers progressives to educate themselves about antisemitism?

This specific debate, I want to stress, is important not just because of the size of California or the precedent that its decision may ultimately set across America, but also because it so effectively encapsulates the dynamics of erasure that Mizrahi Jews face every day. Emily Benedek is not a fringe voice. Her article was lauded by Bari Weiss, one of the biggest centrist Jewish voices today and author of *How to Fight Anti-Semitism*, as well as many other leading voices in Jewish advocacy today.

"The crime here," Benedek writes in her author's note in *Tablet*, "appears to be that I dared to surface the views of ordinary Jews."

On this point, I agree with her. This resistance to any recognition of Mizrahi Jews—let alone acknowledging the unique forms of oppression we face—is all too ordinary.

Jewish advocates are not the only people who have opposed including Mizrahim in the curriculum, however. I am sure Benedek had no intention of linking arms with the worst anti-Israel advocates, but sure enough, there was also a backlash to the JIMENA-influenced curriculum from those who hate Israel. From their perspective, Mizrahim are not a real group at all—they are just Arabs bearing a false, colonialist label imposed by the Ashkenazi hegemony in Israel.

And so it was that anti-Israel advocates such as Linda Sarsour, Noura Erakat, and the far-Left anti-Zionist publication *Jewish Currents* also staunchly opposed the inclusion of Mizrahim in the ethnic studies curriculum.

In response to the revisions to the curriculum, Linda Sarsour's advocacy group, MPower Change, launched a formal campaign called "Defend Ethnic Studies." They urged their supporters to write to the California Department of Education and demand they not pass the new draft. In their campaign, they refer to the revisions as "sabotage."

Another critic was Noura Erakat, a Palestinian American professor at Rutgers University. She is one of the most well-respected faces of the anti-Israel movement.

Following the inclusion of the JIMENA-endorsed curriculum, Erakat railed against the changes, tweeting that she believed "...that an emancipatory Ethnic Studies curriculum, including Arab American Studies, is necessary for dismantling white supremacy & charting decolonial futures."[7] Even though nothing had been stripped of the Arab American section other than calls for anti-Israel boycotts, non-Arabic Middle Eastern minorities, such as my family, were added in.

More criticism of the revised curriculum came from *Jewish Currents*, which published a February 2021 piece by Gabi Kirk, a research assistant at the University of California, Davis. Kirk argued that that the new curriculum focused too heavily on the antisemitism that Mizrahi Jews have experienced and not enough on Islamophobia and anti-Arab sentiment. Kirk claimed:

> Yet the lesson plan contains few resources or examples of "experiences of discrimination" apart from antisemitism—meaning it does not mention anti-Arab racism or Islamophobia. Shahar Zaken, a graduate student in sociology at University of California Davis and longtime Mizrahi community organizer, argues that the discrimination Mizrahim face in the US cannot be covered by a curriculum that "deliberately eras[es] Islamophobia from the conversation": The racial profiling and stigmatization that Mizrahim experience is of a piece with the treatment of Arab immigrants writ large. "Every Jewish Mizrahi that lives in America that looks Arab...has had an experience of Islamophobia," he explained.[8]

Though it may sound plausible, this message is carefully crafted to erase and replace unique Mizrahi experiences with Muslim ones. When I told my Iraqi grandmother—the one who lived through the Farhud—that a handful of American

Jews have insinuated that she and her family were denaturalized, dispossessed, and expelled from Iraq because of Islamophobia and anti-Arab bigotry, she was floored. Of course, they were expelled as Jews precisely because they were *not* Muslim or Arab.

Similar arguments are never used to characterize other religious minorities from the Middle East, yet Mizrahim are consistently told by the anti-Zionist Left that we were all actually Arabs, and only now are we "subjected to antisemitism." The reality is that a brown-skinned Mizrahi Jew is likely to be stopped by airport security in America, and other Western countries, even if he is wearing a kippah and a big Star of David necklace. And guess what? The unique prejudice Mizrahi Jews experience is not made any easier by the fact that it doesn't fit in whatever box some people may find politically convenient.

What's remarkable about this all is that figures as ideologically opposed as Emily Benedek and Linda Sarsour were able to unite around one single cause: keeping Mizrahi Jewish history out of schools.

The big question, for me at least, is why. What secret buttons does Mizrahi identity push, such that so many people want it to go away? Some Jews on the Right, I think, see our inclusion as a threat to their own centrality in the narrative of Jewish suffering. They fear that we will be perceived as more oppressed—because we experience both racism and antisemitism. That somehow the recognition of the horrors we experienced might steal the light from those that occurred to Ashkenazi Jews. *For some Jews, Mizrahi suffering is a distraction from Ashkenazi suffering.*

On the anti-Zionist Left, on the other hand, the buttons are easier to see. The erasure of Mizrahim makes it easier to paint Jews as foreign, colonialist invaders of the Middle East, to whitewash the crimes against humanity committed against Jews in the Middle East and thereby preserve the "good guy" status of the Arab and Muslim world, and to deny Jewish nationhood, which is a prerequisite for denying the legitimacy of Israel.

Many anti-Israel activists indeed go as far as to claim explicitly that our whole identity is fake. A search for the word *Mizrahim* on the Al Jazeera website will yield an article from 2017 called simply "Invention of the Mizrahim," in which Susan Abulhawa, a Palestinian American novelist and activist, explains how "Israel invented the word Mizrahim to strip Arab Jews of their histories as they tried to do with Palestinians." No Mizrahi Jews were quoted in the piece, of course, and for a good reason: the term *Mizrahim* makes me and countless others feel that our own history is acknowledged. We were a people without a name for so long, and now we have one—and it drives people crazy.

So instead, they call us Arab Jews. But they, not Israel, are the ones trying to strip us of our identity—in the process erasing the distinction between us and those who oppressed us, thereby exonerating our oppressors and removing our legitimacy as an ethnicity and peoplehood. By refusing to acknowledge that Jews of the Middle East were in fact a separate people across the Muslim world, with inferior status and subject to systemic and often violent oppression *because we were Jews*, it paves the way to negating not only us but also the Jewish state of which we are the largest ethnic component.

Historically, Muslim regimes explicitly did *not* deem Mizrahi Jews to be Arab. As such, the government treated Jews less than equal under the law. Jews could not ride horses, be at eye-level with Muslims, bear arms, or testify against Muslims in court. They were forbidden from building synagogues as high as mosques, breaking curfew, or even dressing without imposed Jewish symbols. And then there was the protection money: Mizrahim were forced to pay a tax not to be murdered or pillaged.

No, there was no equality, no paradise for Jews in Arab lands. Calling Mizrahi Jews Arab is revising history in the most offensive way imaginable. In the effort to promote an "Arab American" narrative, it seeks to erase the inequalities our ancestors faced at the hands of their ancestors, all in order to falsely paint Israel as a White-supremacist implant.

This is why educating about Mizrahi history is so important. If we can show how Mizrahim were denied a nationality outside our Jewishness in the Middle East, that will help create a foundation for the Jewish national identity of Israelis. It justifies why we need a country of our own.

Anti-Israel advocates know this, so they seek to classify all Jews solely as a form of religion. No religion, the argument goes, is entitled to a country; that is just a theocracy. (The fact that many anti-Zionists have no qualms with the existence of Muslim theocratic nations is beside the point.) The self-determination of oppressed peoples is a fundamental progressive principle, and Israel was founded with exactly that purpose—so erasing Mizrahim is how they square the circle.

Noura Erakat herself subscribes to these very principles. She explains best how rejecting Judaism as ethnicity and painting it solely as a religion serves anti-Israel advocacy, as she tweeted: "Palestinians & their allies have been preaching for 100+ yrs that Zionism is a political project & Judaism is a religion. Zionists have worked at highest levels to equate them to excuse/sustain Israeli violence. Combat antisemitism by joining us in insisting upon this difference."[9]

Yes, Judaism is a religion. But it is also a nation—and has been since time immemorial—and I believe that all nations are inherently political, craving the tools of sanctuary and self-determination. This principle is the basis of contemporary Zionism.

I think the Right-wing Jewish critics, those who call my arguments "divisive," would share all of these values. In fact, in my years as a speaker in the pro-Israel space, there has been a lot of desire for me to speak about my family's experience as Jews in the Middle East. Many of them welcome my talking about our history—as long as it is strictly framed as pro-Israel or an attack on Arabs.

Which brings me back to Emily Benedek. Although she was so adamant that acknowledging Mizrahim was inappropriately dividing Jews into subgroups, she herself has capitalized on our history when it furthered her own agenda.

Like so many who would find even the term *Jew of color* problematic, Benedek has been perfectly willing to acknowledge unique Jewish ethnic identities so long as she can weaponize it against anti-Zionists, mainly Arabs. Just one year before her *Tablet* piece, she wrote at length about Mizrahi history for *Mosaic* as an avenue to rail against the antisemitism we faced at the hands of the Arab world.

Jews who stand against the inclusion of Mizrahi history, however, play right into the hands of anti-Zionists, who are also desperate to erase us.

I will say it again: empowering the voices of Mizrahi Jews will empower the entire Jewish people.

On the other hand, crushing Mizrahi stories, erasing our history, and painting our calls for inclusion as "divisive" gives support to the arguments of the antisemites.

Recognizing Mizrahim helps all Jews. We were denied Arab national identity in exactly the same way that Jews in Eastern Europe were denied the right to be German or Polish. This designation was the basis of our systemic discrimination, denial of our civil rights, dispossession, and mass murder across the globe, from Bia ystok to Baghdad. This shared heritage shows how all Jews were systematically forced to become a borderless nation—*and why we had to build our own.*

Mizrahi Jews also are living proof that Jews are indigenous to the Middle East. Although all Jews have roots in the Land of Israel, many of our people were forced to migrate around the world. Mizrahi Jews, whether we come from Iraq or Jerusalem, are proof that Jews come from the region; we just never left. Our communities are some of the most ancient.

I am a proud descendant of Babylonian Jews who have lived in the area since 586 BCE. Our ancestors are Jews of the ancient Kingdom of Judah, whom Nebuchadnezzar II, the second king of the Neo-Babylonian Empire, exiled from the Land of Israel. While so many seek to deny the endless archaeological evidence that shows Jewish ties to Israel, it is much harder to deny that actual people live in these regions due to that history.

Finally, Mizrahi Jews can play a constructive role in progressive circles that too often have missed the mark with respect to antisemitism. Again, one of the shortcomings of modern social justice movements is the lack of nuance they show when addressing oppression. While the terminology for advocacy has gotten more complex, the outlook has become more simplistic. The only forms of oppression activists recognize in too many movements are race, gender, and sexuality. Antisemitism is none of those, as Jewish identity encompasses so many things; it sits at the intersection of faith, ethnicity, nationality, and peoplehood—and race, depending on whose definition of Whiteness you're using. But it is not difficult to show that antisemitism is real, that people have historically hated Jews and expressed it through different forms of oppression and violence, and that antisemitism continues to be a real problem today. If Mizrahi Jews can get into the room, as JIMENA did, and be received as people of color—therefore worthy of protection—we can use that recognition to educate others on antisemitism.

Uplifting Mizrahi Jews is uplifting all Jews. What does it matter what kinds of Jews are advocating for a better understanding of antisemitism? If the definition of antisemitism is in the curriculum, that makes us all safer. If the next generation is taught that all Jews originate from the Middle East, that we face oppression and violence and need protection, that makes us all safer. I wish that fighting antisemitism was considered essential learning for everyone. However, we know that is simply not true. But if we instill an understanding of what it means to be Jewish in the next generation, it will be.

In the meantime, we must all condemn this monstrous lie that Mizrahim don't exist, and the implicit claim being made that Jews from Arab lands are just too dumb to know who they "really" are. No one—Right or Left, Zionist or anti-Zionist, Jewish or non-Jewish—has a right to tell us who we are, or to deny our right to claim our identity, our history, and our cultural commonality. There is no justification for white-washing the antisemitic murder of my great-grandfather, the expulsion of my grandmother, and the violent oppression we endured, whether at the hands of Vichy occupiers or Iraqi mobs, for the singular crime of being Jews.

Those who silence us, who attempt to erase our very identity, who refuse to acknowledge the Mizrahi story—whether in the California schools or in the US House of Representatives or within Israel itself—are guilty of the very same transgressions they so vehemently decry in other cases. Keeping Mizrahim quiet demonstrates the ugly truth that those who preach the doctrine of intersectionality, diversity, and inclusion, but fail to live up to its ideals, undermine the progressive movement as a whole and are a threat to its long-term viability. We will never be able to convince people in power that we must be heard if we cannot hear each other first.

Mizrahi Jews are real. No one will erase us.

Mizrahi Jews are not Ashkenazi Jews.

Throughout this book, I have attempted to describe the general experience of Mizrahim. While the experience of Christian and Jewish Americans is similar in many ways, it is also very different. The same can be said for Mizrahi Jews:

while our experience is similar to that of Ashkenazi Jews, it is also very different. We have developed a specific identity from living in the Arab and Muslim world for centuries. We have a shared memory and a shared cultural inheritance, and while it may not be identical for all Mizrahim, our overall story connects us.

When unique groups face hate and the threat of real danger, much like the Jewish community in America has, they come together. We should always be united as one Jewish people, but we must also make room for Mizrahi Jews to share our history and to advocate for our interests.

We also cannot ignore the Western conversation about race. We cannot claim racism does not exist or that critical race theory is an antisemitic concept that was formulated to harm Jews, because it is not true. Far too many Jews have tried to ignore or demonize these concepts. Many of them, especially white-skinned Ashkenazi Jews in America, try to claim "all Jews are people of color."

When I speak with such people, I often ask them if they recognize that not all Jews are Black Jews. On this, they usually agree. I then ask if they recognize that Black Jews have a different experience from that of non-Black Jews, which they also can't deny. Given these realities, how could one argue that brown-skinned, Middle Eastern–looking Jews with Arabic-sounding names have the same experience as someone with fair skin and an American Ashkenazi name? When the question is put that way, they typically shut down the conversation or tell me I focus too much on what divides us. On one occasion, someone even sent me a photo of themselves with a spray tan in response.

This was the case in 2020 when I organized a first-of-its-kind online panel discussion about antisemitism. Instead of inviting the usual pundits to speak about Jewish identity, I decided to invite four Jews of color: Mexican American Jewish state representative Alma Hernandez from Arizona, Ethiopian Israeli Jewish leader Ashager Araro, Tewa organizer Mahrinah Shije, and Rabbi Sandra Lawson, who is African American.

One Jewish leader emailed me to say that while they appreciated what I was trying to do with this panel, I should have also included Ashkenazi Jews. I replied that the panel did include an Ashkenazi Jew. Rabbi Sandra follows Ashkenazi tradition and is a director in the Reconstructionist movement. "That's not what I meant," the person wrote back. At that moment, I realized that for some American Jews, being Black makes one insufficiently Ashkenazi. The subtext of the letter was that I should have brought in a Jew with pale skin. Put more starkly, this individual used "Ashkenazi" as a politically correct stand-in for "white-skinned."

Ashkenazi and Mizrahi are not racial identities. Blackness and Ashkenazi heritage are not opposites. The same goes for Mizrahi—although all of us originated from the Middle East Diaspora, we are a multitude of races. The Jews of Kaifeng,

China, originate from Iran, so they are Asian and Mizrahi. Sephardic communities cross racial lines as well; while many Sephardi Jews are from Latin America or North Africa, many others are white-skinned with origins from Spain and Portugal.

I've argued a lot that Mizrahim share a heritage and identity, but I also believe the same goes for me and Rabbi Sandra. We are both Jews of color. We both experience racism in addition to antisemitism and have shared experiences within and outside the Jewish community. Neither of us will see our faces as the "default Jew" on a Jewish holiday card, and Jews like us rarely appear in movies or on television.

I believe that embracing this shared identity as Jews of color unites many of us and gives us a voice.

I also cannot fail to acknowledge that Jews of color have a wide range of experiences. Anti-blackness functions differently than anti-Middle Eastern prejudice, and the challenges that Asian Jews and Latin American Jews face are different from mine. While we all face unique prejudices, we share the experience of being excluded within the Jewish community on the basis of our race, and outside of it on the basis of our Jewishness.

However, I think what unites us is enough for a kind of societal "collective bargaining." Together, Jews of color can push back on how we are underrepresented. We can speak up about how so many of us are perceived as not Jewish enough when we walk into a Jewish space. We can advocate for the end of a "default Jew" in the media and in our households.

It is in the best interest of Mizrahim to identify as Jews of color and to deliberately join forces with that community. However, we must overcome major obstacles to get there. The first is colorism. While some Mizrahim are very dark-skinned, others have lighter complexions. The hatred of us is often racialized, but also rooted in orientalism—how other Jews talk down our food, language, and traditions.

The second issue is that Mizrahi Jews, particularly those in Israel, have adopted a very Right-wing political outlook. This has caused a schism between us and many other Jews of color, who primarily lean Left on the political spectrum. It's important to understand that this is an outcome of our specific traumas. Since most Jews of the Middle East have been brutalized and exiled from Arab countries, they tend to be very hawkish in their approach toward Hamas, the Palestinian Authority, Iran, and those Arab states that support terror against Israel. For young Mizrahim, we are at war with the very people who murdered and expelled our grandparents. The animosity is deep. I've found that this sentiment stretches far beyond Israel and includes my Mizrahi friends in Los Angeles and Great Neck.

In Israel, Mizrahi Jews have consistently voted for parties on the Right, and especially Likud, based solely on the conflict. Likud, however, has done little to amend the disparities that Mizrahim experience in education and income and has rarely promoted Mizrahi politicians to the highest levels.

There are signs this may change, however. In an August 2021 interview with Israel's largest newspaper, Miri Regev, the Moroccan Jewish former Likud minister and current member of the Knesset, promised to campaign to replace Netanyahu while emphasizing her ethnic heritage. "Mizrahi Likudniks voted over the years for 'white people' to lead them," she said. "I think the day after Bibi Netanyahu, Likudniks will have to [do] some soul-searching...if Likudniks continue to elect leaders with 'white' DNA, a new Likud will arise.... There will be a real Sephardi Likud that will express the Sephardi voice that has been quieted for years."[10]

Taking it a step further, Regev called the new government (then) of former prime minister Naftali Bennett and former foreign minister Yair Lapid "an Ashkenazi elitist clique."

Though I don't believe inflammatory rhetoric like this will do much to bring change, it's worth recognizing that politicians are speaking out about Mizrahi absence from real political leadership in Israel.

To me the most compelling part of Regev's interview was how she described her reaction to the election of Barack Obama as president of the United States in 2008. She compared the Mizrahi struggle to the African American civil rights movement, noting that Mizrahim have done menial labor for Ashkenazim over the years, much like Black voters have done for Democrats in America. The feeling of a marginalized group breaking through from the voting base, to actually becoming the people in power, resonated deeply with her: "When Obama was elected, I sat and cried for an hour in front of the television," she said. "When I saw movies and read books on the slavery of [Black Americans] and about Black women having to sit in the back of the bus, it hurt me, because where I come from makes me care about justice."[11]

Though I would not call the treatment of Mizrahi Jews comparable to Jim Crow, we do have a history of discrimination, underrepresentation, dispossession, and being sidelined from leadership roles. Mizrahim are rarely the face of major institutions where our community has large numbers, whether in Israel or in Los Angeles. It is not shocking to me then that an Israeli Mizrahi politician would be so invested in a breakthrough for Black representation in America; it's because we share a community with all people of color, particularly other Jews of color.

My call for Mizrahim to embrace that we are Jews of color thus is not rooted in tribalism and divisiveness, but in a sense of empathy and community. We all know how meaningful it is to see a person of color in power, to know that we too can be the face of Jews or even just a face of Jews. It doesn't just have to be the prime minister of Israel. I cannot begin to imagine the impact it would have on my community if we saw a person of color become the executive director of the ADL

(Anti-Defamation League), the Conference of Presidents, or the Union for Reform Judaism. The message should be that there is no glass ceiling on the opportunities for my children within the Jewish community.

Nor am I advocating for Jews of color to replace white-skinned Jews in the so-called hierarchy. I'm calling for an end to the hierarchy altogether. Today, we do not have a seat at the table. But if we work together, as Jews of color, we can and we will pull up a chair.

What really is a Jew of color?

In May 2019 a study entitled "Counting Inconsistencies: An Analysis of American Jewish Population Studies with a Focus on Jews of Color," stated that "Jews of Color represent at least 12%–15% of American Jews."[12] The study—conducted by researchers from the University of San Francisco, Stanford University, and the Jews of Color Initiative—found that data on this subject in America is inconsistent. Some studies did not ask about race or ethnicity at all, while other studies sampled respondents in ways that likely undercounted Jews of color. "Questions about race and ethnicity were not comparable across studies and often confused multiple types of identity. Employing nonstandard questions also created mismatches with reference surveys used to weigh Jewish population estimates."

It was, in other words, a mess.

Earlier, I presented the definition of Jews of color as it relates to the definition of people of color, but in America, many understand the term *Jews of Color* as referring only to Black Jews.

However, from its inception, the term *Jews of Color* was meant to include a much broader range. It first appeared in print in a 2001 issue of *Bridges: A Journal for Jewish Feminists and Our Friends*. The issue was dedicated to "Writing and Art by Jewish Women of Color." Shahanna McKinney-Baldon, a Black Jewish leader from the Bay Area with years of experience in Jewish advocacy, wrote the introduction, in which she coined the term.

"This collection of writings and artwork by Jewish women of color—Jewish women of African, Asian, Latin, and Native American heritages—offers readers a chance to think about racism within the Jewish community," she wrote. "How we name ourselves and our experiences is a place to begin."

Nineteen years later, McKinney-Baldon wrote an essay about how, in recent times, she has become troubled by a growing amount of confusion surrounding the term *Jews of Color*. Her goal, she wrote, had been to create a term that would help make Jewish communities more welcoming and inclusive.

"The idea for the *Bridges* issue came into being in the late 1990s, when progressives placed great value on multicultural coalitions. '[The term] "people of color" created a basis to do coalition-building among all people targeted by racism as nonwhites,'"[13] McKinney-Baldon wrote in 2020.[14]

She added that using the term *Jews of Color* was meant to introduce people's minds to the idea that some Jews might be targeted by racism because their recent background is other than European, but also pointed out that employing the term can be a political act.

The term, in other words, was introduced in order to help foster a coalition, not to exclude anyone. It enabled Jews who share similar experiences of oppression for their racial identity to connect and act together. It is also a tool to educate non-Jews about the diversity of our community.

And yet, not everything is about racism. Jews can be the target of antisemitism no matter how white their skin—just as gays can experience homophobia no matter the color of their skin. I have witnessed, in certain Jewish circles, a conversation about Jews as a race, which just makes my skin crawl. I think that some Jews in the West, and particularly those on the political Right, are so mired in what's been called the "Oppression Olympics" that they equate hatred of Jews with racism. In other words, they try to replace the term *antisemitism* with *anti-Jewish racism*.

McKinney-Baldon also explained that "the term was indeed used mindfully by its early adopters—it was our call for a new coalition." She continued, "It was a tool that we used to crack open the door to conversations about racial and ethnic 'minority within a minority' experiences in Jewish communities."

She added that it was giving recognition to the idea that one "cannot totally disentangle the Eurocentrism in our US Jewish communities from the Eurocentrism in the wider world, nor the various varieties of contemporary American xenophobia from the eternal specter of American racism."

Growing up in Israel, I did not have these linguistic tools at my disposal. Although English is my third language, I can better communicate my feelings of belonging, racial identity, and Jewishness in English than I can in Hebrew. We simply do not have the terminology to identify this shared experience. There is no such thing as a "Jew of color" in Israel. We do not see the Mizrahi community as intertwined with the Ethiopian or Indian Jews around us. However, I believe that such a term can be a means of empowerment and expression in Israel just as much as in America.

What defines Jews of color in America is being Jewish and non-White while facing both erasure from the Jewish community and systemic racism. The recognition of this commonality creates a bond. For instance, while Latin American Jews haven't faced oppression in the Muslim world, they do face racism. And while neither Mizrahi nor Latin American Jews face the same kind of racism as Black Jews face, the experience can still form a bond among them.

When people are not separated into subgroups, they have more power and can reclaim their dignity. I admire the way we come together as Jews to fight antisemitism and preserve our shared traditions. We Jews of color must unite to recognize what we share as we stand at the intersection of racism and antisemitism. And we Mizrahim—whether Moroccan, Libyan, Syrian, Persian, or Yemenite in our origins—must similarly join forces.

The Jewish people are a family, and we each hold more immediate families in our clan. Brothers share a different connection than cousins, but at the end of the day, we are all seated at the same Shabbat table.

When I first moved to the United States and joined a community of American Jews, I struggled to identify with them. I realized that their culture felt so foreign to me largely because of the absence of Mizrahi influence. In Israel, Mizrahi heritage is present in our music, food, and dance. This is not the case in most American Jewish communities.

However, I still found ways to feel seen. That occurred most often with other American Jews who felt as invisible as I did—Black Jews, Asian Jews, and Latin American Jews. I also found a home in the LGBTQ community. I was able to identify with disabled and autistic Jews and with Ashkenazi Jews who felt excluded from progressive movements because of their profound support for Israel.

That's the thing about ghosts—we can see each other.

———◆◆◆———

Perhaps because I see myself as a progressive activist, I am most deeply concerned about progressive antisemitism. Unlike far-Right antisemitism, which is no less abhorrent or lethal, progressive antisemitism makes hatred of Jews culturally acceptable.

Progressive antisemites paint Jews as omnipresent oppressors. Instead of holding back society as a whole—or the White race as White nationalists would assert—progressives use the same stereotypes to hold Jews responsible for capitalism, war, and social inequalities, particularly racism. We are, in other words, the source of the evil they see themselves as fighting against.

While I won't unpack this complicated dynamic, I can say that antisemitic progressivism is a nightmare for me as a Jew of color. I need the advocacy of progressive movements to upend the forms of prejudice I experience. Antisemitism on the Left is catastrophic for Jewish people for the simple reason that we desperately need partners in bringing down the far-Right antisemites who shoot up our synagogues and steal our lives. If the activists who call out White supremacists for threatening our freedoms have their own implicit biases against Jews, or even a blind spot to the antisemitism in their midst, we lose a great deal of our inherent collective power.

Jews are outnumbered and will always be outnumbered. But if the progressive movement develops concern and empathy for the Jewish people, we will be significantly less isolated.

It has been one of my missions the past few years to push for change within progressive causes. I find that callouts and outrage (which I admit I use often) are not the most helpful tools for changing the dynamics we encounter. A face-to-face connection, empathy, and moral courage can change an antisemite into an advocate for the Jewish people.

So when someone in the public eye engages in antisemitism—which usually stems from ignorance, not hatred—my first instinct is to reach out to them in a compassionate way. I ask if we can have a candid conversation about antisemitism. I address them as humans rather than faceless bigots. And I try to reach a point of mutual understanding and growth.

Often, those I engage with in this capacity are people of color who have said something deeply insensitive about Jewish people, typically cloaked in progressive or anti-racist vernacular.

This dynamic played directly into a conversation I once had with fashion designer Recho Omondi. She faced backlash for making charged statements about Jewish women on her podcast called *The Cutting Room Floor*. In an interview with Leandra Medine Cohen, a Jewish blogger, Omondi called her guest a "Jewish American Princess." Taking another jab at Medine Cohen's heritage, she added, "At the end of the day you guys are going to get your nose jobs and your keratin treatments and change your last name from Ralph Lifshitz to Ralph Lauren, and you will be fine."[15] This statement, along with her false comment that Jews played an outsized role in the slave trade, quickly drew criticism from the Jewish community.

Primarily, the issue is that Omondi had invoked antisemitic stereotypes in her attempt to call out her guest's entitlement and privilege. Her potentially noble quest to fight certain inequalities fell apart because she participated in another form of prejudice. Facing outcry from the Jewish community, she issued what I feel was a heartfelt apology.

Medine Cohen is a Mizrahi woman of half-Turkish and half-Iranian descent. But Omondi did not know that. She did not even know Jews originated from those regions.

So I reached out to her. During our heart-to-heart conversation, Omondi explained to me that as a Black woman growing up in America, she didn't know about Jews of color. In her middle-class upbringing, Omondi was only exposed to what she described as wealthy white girls who randomly dropped the fact they were Jewish only in the middle of a conversation after years of knowing them. Omondi was puzzled by how these Jewish women were not openly proud of their ethnicity, heritage, and identity. I used this as an opportunity to talk about assimilation and how erasing one's Jewishness became a survival tactic in the West, passed down through the generations. This history clicked with her experience of code-switching to be accepted by her White peers.

We then discussed the need to bridge the gap between non-Jewish and Jewish people of color. Omondi told me that if she only had known Jews of color existed and that they cannot just assimilate into the White majority, nor do they want to, she would have had a different view of the Jewish community. It would have challenged the stereotypes she believed about Jews as a whole.

Let me be clear, however: the rhetoric Omondi used was unacceptable, whether aimed at a Mizrahi or Ashkenazi woman. Antisemitism is vile and lethal regardless of the target. In no way are Jews of color "the good ones" or worthy of extra protection. But my experience as a Jew of color did, however, create an opportunity to speak to Omondi in a way that others perhaps could not.

I wish we lived in a world where we could easily teach people that bigotry against anyone is wrong, even if it is borne out of your personal traumas or bad experiences with one member of a particular community. I wish that unpacking antisemitism was as easy as just calling it out and condemning it. Many people approached Omondi with that outlook. They publicly lambasted her, went after her reputation, and tried to shame her into apologizing.

Those tools might be effective in some cases. And the recrimination against antisemitism is of course justified.

However, I'm not looking just to punish people for expressing bias against Jews. I don't just want to build a society where it is socially unacceptable to express antisemitic beliefs. I want to *end* antisemitism, which is a far more difficult task. That means fundamentally changing the outlooks of millions of people and helping them unlearn conspiracy theories and stereotypes that have persisted for thousands of years.

The trope Omondi participated in ("Jewish American Princess") is something that even Jewish communities themselves have upheld. Male Jewish novelists of the midcentury—men like Philip Roth, Saul Bellow, and J. D. Salinger—are arguably the ones who created the sexist perception of Jewish women. In my lifetime, I've often heard other Jewish girls refer to each other as a "JAP."

While many activists and organizations have worked hard to unpack and end antisemitism in mainstream society, I do not think we have created a strategy to reach out to communities of color and educate them about Jews. Perhaps it is because as people of color, we already have our wings clipped by the racism we experience. We assume that our fellow people of color are powerless to commit significant damage against us. Some on the far Left even make the argument that we cannot call out antisemitism from people of color at all. This is as absurd as it is racist.

We've seen how antisemitism from people of color can become lethal, from the Monsey Chanukah party stabbing to the Jersey City kosher supermarket shooting to the Crown Heights riots. This reality is acutely obvious in Israel, where most Israelis and Palestinians are of the same skin color. Antisemites, acting in the name of anti-Zionism, have stabbed random Jews on the streets and blown up buses and ice cream parlors. The entrenched hatred of Jews in the region, many centuries in the making, is a long-standing obstacle to meaningful peace.

However, many fail to recognize that the primary victims of antisemitism in communities of color are Jews like me. We are sometimes unwelcome on account of our Judaism, just as in some Jewish spaces we are isolated because of our race. This ignorance affects our day-to-day lives and puts us in a place of communal homelessness.

Yet I believe that Jews of color are uniquely qualified to bridge these gaps and end antisemitism of the Left altogether within the broader movements for social and racial equality.

For this reason, Mizrahim should not just identify as Jews of color, but as people of color within the broader movement for racial equality. As the largest population of Jews of color, we are in a unique position to combat misconceptions about Jews and Israel.

Unfortunately, many Mizrahim today do not identify as people of color within justice movements. We see ourselves as simply Jewish or Mizrahi, mainly because these movements have never catered to our needs or invited us to the table as partners. That's not to say that Mizrahim aren't active in fighting racial injustice. We are not absent in marches for ending racism and police brutality, for gender equality, or for LGBTQ liberation.

But Mizrahi Jews must embrace that we are people of color and join movements for racial justice, not strictly as allies or as peers, but potentially as leaders. This shift would empower us to fight both the racism we experience and the antisemitism we detest. Imagine if we could have these vulnerable conversations about Judaism, race, and oppression on a more regular basis instead of only after someone gets called out for a transgression.

Such a transformation in our identity has its challenges. Middle Eastern people don't fall neatly into Western racial dynamics. For decades, the American census categorized Middle Eastern people as White, even though we are neither physically nor culturally so. After a lot of advocacy and determined lobbying, many organizations have started to list Middle Eastern as its own ethnicity.

Colorism also plays a role. While many Mizrahim have dark skin tones, quite a few of us are White-passing, especially after not getting enough sun. As a result, I would never claim to face the same challenges as a dark-skinned Black man. But as we all know, race has always been a social construct, rooted neither in genetics nor skin color. Racism has always centered around oppression. It is about where you exist in the hierarchy, not actually what you look like.

Many progressive spaces have already recognized Middle Easterners as non-White. Muslims from the region, in particular, strongly identify as people of color. This phenomenon has led to stronger alliances and increased solidarity against Islamophobia. Mizrahim now have an opportunity to do the same. When we show up for racial justice for ourselves and others, more people will start showing up for Jews.

Since I moved to London to live with my British partner, Marc, I realized that not all mothers behave the same. Marc's mother cares for and loves her son deeply. My mother loves me too, of course, but demonstrates it by calling me two, three, and sometimes four times a day to make sure I am still alive. She expects me to send text messages and location updates constantly even though we live on different continents. Indeed, the stereotype of the overbearing Jewish mother is not lost on me. Yet many of my Ashkenazi friends have told me that their moms are not as intense as mine.

I've noticed things about my Ashkenazi peers too. In my extended family, which is truly outsized as each of my grandparents has around ten siblings, who each have three to four children, on average, we never cut each other out. On the other hand, in many families, people aren't in contact with each other in order to avoid emotional and other kinds of abuse. However, even as we age and it becomes less acceptable to call our mother four times a day, the level of contact in my family is consistent, and certain boundaries just don't exist.

One thing that Mizrahim can teach other communities is not necessarily how to love your family, but *how to trust* your family and, fundamentally, how to trust the concept of family.

When you visit a Mizrahi family's home, you will be hugged. If you have gained weight, you will be notified of that fact before immediately being seated at the dining table and ordered to eat more food—and there is so much of it, and it is very good. At a Mizrahi home, there may also be shouting, laughter, and unapologetic ideas. We are not passive-aggressive, we are aggressive. If you were to visit an Italian or Puerto Rican family, it perhaps would be a similar feeling. If you are disliked, you will know it. But if you are loved, you will not be able to escape the embrace and support from all directions. You will know that this is your foundation—if everything else in the world crumbles, it will hold you up no matter what.

The Mizrahi family is also often politically Right wing. They are nationalists who care about their country's survival and security. They probably keep kosher and attend synagogue on Shabbat. You will notice that these families have many children. It may even come as a surprise that, despite their hawkish nature, Mizrahi parents embrace their kids regardless of their sexual identities or political beliefs. I know this for a fact because I was one of them. In fact, the Mizrahi family will fight for their queer children because the only thing we haven't lost is each other.

The Mizrahi origin story is tragic, but it functions very differently from that of our Ashkenazi brothers and sisters, particularly those ravaged by the Holocaust. One of the most harrowing practices that the Nazis engaged in was selections. When Jews arrived at concentration camps, the first thing the guards did was physically tear families apart. They were separated into two lines: one to live, another to die.

This practice is beyond words, but I think the following account from Holocaust survivor Jack Kagan best paints the grim picture. This is his experience at a concentration camp before he escaped and joined the Bielski partisans, a Nazi resistance group that later became the focus of the film *Defiance*:

> Early morning, lorries arrived, the doors have opened, the Nazi arrived and started a selection. You came out, he asked you, the head of the family, your profession, how many children. To the left, it's to go out to the yard; to the right it's to stand in the corner of the entrance of the building.... To the right. That means it was no rhyme or reason whom to select to death and whom to life.

> Because he went in front, two children, saddle maker, the same profession. We were the lucky ones, he left us to remain alive, and them to death. So my uncles Moishke, Soshke, Berol, and Leizer went out

to the yard. They sent out four and a half thousand, four thousand people on lorries, took them outside the town into graves, into prepared graves, and massacred them.

That was Einsatzkommando, that was Einsatzkommando. My mother was standing practically opposite the window, and suddenly out of nowhere police, SS, came, with the back of their rifles hitting everybody, and I knew that this is the end of the people which are standing on the yard. In this execution I lost my mother, I lost my sister Nachama, I lost my auntie Surcharsky.[16]

There are countless permutations of this story. Sometimes family members were shot, and sometimes they were gassed. One of the most horrific moments in Elie Wiesel's famous account *Night* is when he describes how he saw his father go to bed, weak from forced labor. When Elie woke up the next day, his father was gone. At that moment, he realized he'd never see his father again.

This experience is not limited to the Holocaust; Jews were taken from their families and dumped in gulags in the former Soviet Union. Nor is it purely an Ashkenazi phenomenon; family separation occurred frequently during the Inquisition when the Catholic Church would abduct Jews and torture them to death.

Many Jews carry, deep down, the belief that when a family member leaves your sight, they might never come back.

So many of our communities have experienced the horrors of antisemites violently ripping our bloodlines apart, from having the baby you are feeding being taken by the Nazis in the middle of the night to having a mother shot in front of her children to having your parents send you off to hide and not seeing them again. This sort of trauma cannot disappear in a generation or two. Even those who didn't experience the Holocaust directly, or who fortunately got out, often have a cousin or a brother or a grandfather who didn't. For too many of us, the only insight we have into our family history is from Nazi deportation records.

This, however, is a point that generally distinguishes Mizrahi Jews and defines our culture: family was the only thing we did not lose. Yes, many of us were murdered, including members of my own family during antisemitic riots. Some Yemenite Jewish children were taken in the early days of Israel's establishment and their fate is still disputed. This loss is unbearable. But for the most part, Mizrahim have a different story, a different relationship to the very idea of family, than other Jewish groups.

When we were second-class citizens in Muslim lands, we did not have dignity, but we had our families. Our basic rights and freedoms were not a given, but Shabbat dinners were.

When antisemitic regimes revoked our passports, seized our land, raped our neighbors, and exiled us from the only countries we'd ever known, Mizrahi Jews escaped through the desert with nothing but our babies on our backs. We crowded on rescue jets, holding nothing but our parents' hands. We huddled in refugee camps and lived in tent cities. It was an absolute poverty of belongings, but not of kin.

My mother doesn't call me several times per day because she is neurotic or worried I might get into danger. She does it because she knows I am the one thing that will always be in her life, regardless of what continent I'm living on. Family is the one irrevocable thing in our existence, and therefore the most precious. I like to use the word *priceless* because it expresses that something's value is infinite. That's what the Mizrahi family is—infinite and, therefore, priceless.

When Mizrahim were forced out of our lands, we left as families. Though some were lost on the way, by and large when we arrived in the UK, America, or Israel, we arrived as one large family unit.

We were just Yemenite, Turkish, Iraqi, Amazigh, Persian, Moroccan, Kurdish, Egyptian, or Libyan when we started the journey, but in the end, we were all Mizrahi. We Mizrahim are Jews of many colors and our love is vivid, saturated with all the shades from the Middle East.

Families are not born, they are built, and ours were crafted out of survival and sand.

There are two groups of non-Mizrahi Jews; one group knows about us, and the other doesn't. But, in my experience, each of these groups seems to ignore our existence. If you've read this far, you are now among the people who know the story of Mizrahi Jews. Having answered every question about Mizrahim that I could possibly imagine, I now ask something of you.

Don't end your engagement with the Mizrahi story when you've finished reading this. I've talked at length about the contradictions in how the world perceives and treats my people. The best way to empower Mizrahi Jews—whether you are one, love one, or have never met one—is to do your part to make this world a little less hypocritical. Fundamentally, our work is to call out the dangerous trends that leave Mizrahim vulnerable and politically homeless.

You cannot claim to care about injustices against Middle Easterners but then ignore the ethnic cleansing of nearly one million Mizrahi Jews.

You cannot be outraged with the current policies of Israel or call us a "colonialist apartheid state that engages in ethnic cleansing" without being furious about Jews in the Middle East who have been treated as second-class citizens for centuries, enduring regular mass killings and institutionalized discrimination at the hands of an expansionist Arab empire.

You cannot be a defender of refugees while ignoring the fact that Israel has been a safe haven for countless innocent refugees who have fled annihilation.

You cannot preach about the importance of an ethic studies curriculum and then actively campaign against teaching Mizrahi heritage.

You cannot claim to stand up for marginalized people but then abandon them when they don't fit your political narrative.

You cannot say that you support Israel—as 95 percent of American Jews do—but then fail to acknowledge or educate yourself about the majority of the citizens who live there.

You cannot serve hummus and pita bread every Friday night at your local Hillel or Chabad without bothering to learn about the various groups who gave Jewish culture its flavor.

You cannot plant trees in Israel, wave our nation's flag in the streets, or call out politicians and celebrities every time they post anti-Zionist tweets but then neglect to advocate for the very communities within its borders.

You cannot lecture about the abuse of Mizrahim at the hands of Arabs and then do nothing to end the inequalities and mistreatment we experience at the hands of our Ashkenazi brothers and sisters.

You cannot boast about how your Jewish organization or community is devoted to diversity just because you've invited Black evangelicals, Pakistani Muslims, and pro-Israel Arabs to speak but then overlook the people of color who are just as Jewish as you are.

You cannot advocate for Zionism out of your love for Jewishness but then see Israel through the eyes of an Evangelical Christian.

You cannot point to the fact that Jews have never been fully accepted into Whiteness and brag about our long history of fighting prejudice but then berate Jews who say they experience racism.

You cannot exclude Mizrahi Jews—and all Jews of color for that matter—from leadership positions within the Jewish community and then claim that you're "welcoming."

You cannot be committed to the idea of Jewish continuity without actively lobbying for Jewish institutions to embrace diversity.

You cannot accept Ashkenazi as a valid Jewish group identity, regardless of differences in French, Russian, and Polish culture only to assert that Mizrahi Jews have no right . to identify collectively.

You cannot promote the notion that the only way to be Jewish is Ashkenazi, or define Jewishness strictly through that lens, while leaving no room for any other heritage to exist, and then brand Mizrahi Jews who present a different heritage as "divisive."

You cannot fully champion the Jewish people when you choose not to see whole sectors of the Jewish people.

We are not asking for much. The somber truth is that some Mizrahim will likely feel uncomfortable reading this. A handful might participate in rhetoric that seeks to repress our stories. They will say that my advocacy for our recognition and respect is bad for the Jewish community. They may claim that we should only focus on what unites us as Jews to the exclusion of Mizrahi heritage. The sad fact is that Mizrahim are so used to receiving nothing that we believe we deserve nothing. A minority of Mizrahim might even push back against this book, saying that we should not ask to be seen by the Jewish community and instead identify as a Jewish minority within the Arab community.

But we are not part of the Arab community. It was the Arab community in the Middle East that made sure we would never forget that. We are proud Jews, and we are Mizrahi.

Our ancestors walked across the desert with tattered shoes and huddled in tents without basic necessities because they knew that we deserve nothing less than full equality, wherever we live.

The generations before us believed that Mizrahi Jews could get full freedom and were willing to do anything to achieve liberation. Now, I'm calling on everyone to follow in their honorable footsteps. I'm calling for unity of the Jewish people, through recognizing our beautiful diversity.

Love Mizrahi Jews as much as you love the food we cook, the music we compose, the history we lived, the country we built, and the soul we gave to her. If you do this, your love will be reciprocated.

ENDNOTES

Chapter I

1. Darcy, Oliver. "CNN severs ties with liberal pundit Marc Lamont Hill after his controversial remarks on Israel," CNN, 30 Nov. 2018, https://edition.cnn.com/2018/11/29/media/marc-lamont-hill-cnn/index.html

2. Frantzman, Seth J. "Marc Lamont Hill Slams Mizrahi Jews as 'Identity Category' of Palestinians," *Jerusalem Post*, 22 May 2019, https://www.jpost.com/arab-israeli-conflict/marc-lamont-hill-slams-mizrahi-jews-as-identity-category-of-palestinians-690349/

3. Sarsour, Linda [@lsarsour]. "Selective memory. Remember the stabbing at the pride parade in Israel? https://www.haaretz.com/2015-07-30/ty-article/6-stabbed-at-jerusalem-gay-pride-parade/0000017f-f780-d044-adff-f7f94aaa0000," Twitter, 10 June, 2017, https://twitter.com/lsarsour/status/873618758060920833

4. Sarsour, Linda [@lsarsour]. "Says the guy who harasses Black Jewish voices on Twitter. Stop it." Twitter.com, undated

5. Gravy, Westside [@WestsideGravy]. "Linda, who are you to speak for Black Jews? We have voices and

are capable of using them. Stop using us to attack leaders like Hen Mazzig who uplift voices that don't fit your narrative, and have defended Black Jews like myself on multiple occasions." Twitter.com, undated

6. Oppenheim, Oren. "Trouble in Hasbara Paradise," *Jerusalem Post,* 28 Aug. 2018, https://www. jpost.com/israel-news/trouble-in-hasbara-paradise-565966; accessed 15 July 2022

7. Sternfeld, Lior, and Arie M. Dubnov. "How did November become the Mizrahi Heritage Month? And what's Mizrahi anyhow?" History News Network, https://historynewsnetwork.org/article/173735

8. Mazzig, Hen. "The real reason Mizrahi Jews support Israel," Israelhayom.com, 12 Aug. 2020, https://www. israelhayom.com/opinions/the-real-reason-mizrahi-jews-support-israel/; accessed 15 July 2022

Chapter 2

1. Derman, Ushi. "Queen of the Desert: The Amazing Story of 'Jewish Khaleesi,'" ANU—Museum of the Jewish People, 14 Oct. 2018, https://www. anumuseum.org.il/blog-items/queen-desert-amazing-story-jewish-khaleesi/; accessed 15 July 2022

2. Genesis 11:1 (English Standard Version)

3. Genesis 11:9 (New King James Version)

4. Psalm 137:1 (New International Version)

Andrews, Mesu. *By the Waters of Babylon: A Captive's Song—Psalm 137* (St. Louis: McPherson Publishing, 2018)

6. Psalm 137:5–6 (King James Version)

7. "World: Death, Diplomacy and Diminishing Peace," *Time*, 7 Feb. 1969, https://content.time.com/time/subscriber/article/0,33009,838918,00.html

8. "1969 Baghdad Hangings," Wikipedia, 7 Dec. 2021, https://en.wikipedia.org/wiki/1969_Baghdad_hangings

9. Makiya, Kanan. *Republic of Fear: The Politics of Modern Iraq* (Berkeley, CA: University of California Press, 1998)

10. Green, David B. "1969: Nine Jewish 'Spies' Are Hanged in Baghdad," *Haaretz*, 27 Jan. 2014, https://www.haaretz.com/2014-01-27/ty-article/.premium/1969-nine-jewish-spies-are-hanged-in-baghdad/0000017f-ea1d-dc91-a17f-fe9d01ec0000

11. Shohat, Ella. *On the Arab-Jew, Palestine, and Other Displacements: Selected Writings of Ella Shohat* (London: Pluto Press, 2017)

12. Aicvideo, director. *Arab-Jews: Interview with Zvi Ben Dor Benite*, YouTube, 3 Aug. 2015, https://www.youtube.com/watch?v=S-3FJX496ds&ab_channel=aicvideo; accessed 12 July 2022

13. Thomas, Bishop. Transcript of Coptic Bishop Thomas's remarks on Egypt's Christians, Hudson Institute, 18 July 2008

14. "Indigenous Peoples," United Nations, Department of Economic and Social Affairs, https://www.un.org/development/desa/indigenouspeoples/about-us.html

15. Mazzig, Hen. "Are Jews Indigenous People? Here's What a Native American Jew Thinks | Opinion," *Newsweek*, 15 Oct. 2020, https://www.newsweek.com/are-jews-indigenous-people-heres-what-native-american-jew-thinks-opinion-1539233

Chapter 3

1. "Anti-Netanyahu Protest Leader Accused of Racism after Comments to Ethiopian Cop," *Times of Israel*, 6 Oct. 2020, https://www.timesofisrael.com/anti-pm-protest-leader-accused-of-racism-after-comments-to-ethiopian-cop/

2. Bitton, Erez. *A Moroccan Gift* (poetry), (Jerusalem: Beit Eked, 1976)

3. Burton, Elise K. *Genetic Crossroads: The Middle East and the Science of Human Heredity* (Redwood City, CA: Stanford University Press, 202)

4. "1972 CIA Document Analyzes Ashkenazi-Sephardic Tensions in Israel," ESefarad, 2 April 2017, https://esefarad.com/?p=76690

5. "Israel: Problems Behind the Battle Lines," US Central Intelligence Agency, intelligence memorandum, 10 May 1972 (released to public 10

Sept. 2010), https://www.cia.gov/readingroom/
docs/CIA-RDP85T00875R001100130058-9.pdf

6. *Menachem Begin Speech Condemning Ma'arach
   Racism,* YouTube, 17 March 2021, https://
   www.youtube.com/watch?v=cL3BEN3oT0E&ab_
   channel=Drion; accessed 13 July 2022

Chapter 4

1. Hillel International and Base. "Racial Justice
   Learn In | Yom Iyyun," Facebook, 23 Aug.
   2020, https://www.facebook.com/events/
   hillel-international/racial-justice-learn-in-yom-
   iyyun/2731961283747510/; accessed 14 July 2022

2. Mishkan Chicago. "Racial Justice Learn In | A Yom
   Iyyun," Mishkan Chicago, 23 Aug. 2020, https://
   www.mishkanchicago.org/event/racial-justice-
   learn-in-a-yom-iyyun/; accessed 14 July 2022

3. Rogan, Seth. Remarks on WTF with Marc Maron
   podcast, 27 July 2020, http://www.wtfpod.com/
   podcast/episode-1143-seth-rogen; accessed 2020

4. Lewin-Epstein, Noah, and Yinon Cohen. "Ethnic
   origin and identity in the Jewish population of Israel,"
   Journal of Ethnic and Migration Studies, vol. 45,
   no. 11, 2018, pp. 2118–2137, https://doi.org/10.1080
   /1369183x.2018.1492370; accessed 14 July 2020

5. al-Gharbi, Musa. "Trump is Doing Surprisingly Well
    with Minority Voters. It Might Not Matter," Gharbi,
    24 Dec. 2020, https://musaalgharbi.com/2020/11/02/
    understanding-trump-success-minority-voters/

6. Landsmann, Carolina. "The Real Reason Mizrahim
    Vote for Netanyahu, and Why the Left Can't Win Them
    Over," *Haaretz*, 11 Jan. 2022, https://www.haaretz.com/
    israel-news/elections/2020-01-11/ty-article-magazine/.
    premium/the-real-reason-mizrahim-vote-for-netanyahu-
    and-why-the-left-cant-win-them-over/0000017f-
    e90c-d62c-a1ff-fd7f5bf90000; accessed 14 July 2020

7. Ibid.

8. Gravé-Lazi, Lidar. "Biton Committee begins work
    to enrich Mizrahi culture in education system,"
    Jerusalem Post, 3 March 2016, https://www.jpost.
    com/israel-news/politics-and-diplomacy/biton-
    committee-begins-work-to-enrich-mizrahi-culture-in-
    education-system-446687; accessed 14 June 2020

9. "The Racist Post by the Senior Publicist Who
    Worked with Begin and Peres," *Maariv*, 11 July 2016,
    https://www.maariv.co.il/landedpages/printarticle.
    aspx?id=548884; accessed 15 July 2022

10. Zagury, Maor. "The White Panthers," *Yediut
    Aharonot*, 14 July 2016, https://www.yediot.co.il/
    articles/0,7340,L-4827847,00.html; accessed 15 July 2022

Chapter 5

1. Mazzig, Hen. "My Grandparents Were Victimized by Nazis. Why Am I Afraid to Call Myself the Grandson of a Survivor?" *Jewish Journal*, June 2020, https://jewishjournal.com/commentary/opinion/317537/my-grandparents-were-victimized-by-nazis-why-am-i-afraid-to-call-myself-the-grandson-of-a-survivor/; accessed 14 June 2020

2. "California's Proposed New Ethnic Studies Curriculum Is Jargon-Filled and All-Too-PC," *Los Angeles Times*, 4 Aug. 2019, https://www.latimes.com/opinion/story/2019-08-02/californias-new-ethnic-studies-curriculum; accessed 15 July 2022

3. Goldstein, Dana. "Push for Ethnic Studies in Schools Faces a Dilemma: Whose Stories to Tell," *New York Times*, 15 Aug. 2019, https://www.nytimes.com/2019/08/15/us/california-ethnic-studies.html; accessed 14 June 2020

4. "Sephardic and Mizrahi Communal Response to the First Draft of Proposed Ethnic Studies Model Curriculum of California's Department of Education," JIMENA, 5 Aug. 2019, https://www.jimena.org/sephardic-and-mizrahi-communal-response-to-the-proposed-ethnic-studies-model-curriculum-of-californias-department-of-education/; accessed 14 June 2020

5. Benedek, Emily [@EmilyBenedek1]. "The whole reason that unit existed was because they could argue they were POC. And then the first source made my skin crawl with Inter-tribal jealousies. Poor all around," Twitter, 29 Jan. 2021, https://twitter.com/emilybenedek1/status/1355326673437286401

6. Benedek, Emily. "California Is Cleansing Jews From History," Tablet, 27 Jan. 2021, https://www.tabletmag.com/sections/news/articles/california-ethnic-studies-curriculum; accessed 14 July 2022

7. Erakat, Noura [@4noura]. "My name is Noura Erakat, Im a faculty member at Rutgers University, New Brunswick and I believe that an emancipatory Ethnic Studies curriculum, including Arab American Studies, is necessary for dismantling white supremacy & charting decolonial futures. #DefendEthnicStudies," Twitter, Jan 12, 2021, https://twitter.com/4noura/status/1349090122461900801

8. Kirk, Gabi. "Authors of California Ethnic Studies Curriculum Decry Cuts to Arab Studies," *Jewish Currents*, 3 Feb. 2021, https://jewishcurrents.org/authors-of-california-ethnic-studies-curriculum-decry-cuts-to-arab-studies; accessed 14 June 2022

9. Erakat, Noura [@4noura] "Palestinians & their allies have been preaching for 100+ yrs that Zionism is a political project & Judaism is a religion. Zionists have worked at

highest levels to equate them to excuse/sustain Israeli violence. Combat antisemitism by joining us in insisting upon this difference," Twitter, 24 May 24 2021, https://twitter.com/4noura/status/1396829212980416513

10. "Miri Regev announces run for prime minister: Stop voting for 'white people,'" *Jerusalem Post*, 15 Aug. 2021, https://www.jpost.com/israel-news/politics-and-diplomacy/miri-regev-announces-run-for-prime-minister-stop-voting-for-white-people-676656; accessed 14 July 2022

11. Sokol, Sam. "Senior Likud Lawmaker Calls on Her Party's Supporters to Stop Electing Leaders With 'White DNA,'" *Haaretz*, 12 Aug. 2021, https://www.haaretz.com/israel-news/2021-08-12/ty-article/.premium/senior-likud-lawmaker-calls-on-her-partys-supporters-to-stop-electing-leaders-with/0000017f-e661-d97e-a37f-f765ce9b0000; accessed 15 July 2022

12. "Counting Inconsistencies from Jews of Color Field Building Initiative," Jim Joseph Foundation, https://jimjosephfoundation.org/news-blogs/population-of-jews-of-color-is-increasing-in-u-s-despite-undercounting-in-population-studies/; accessed 14 July 2022

13. Kelman, Dr. Ari Y, et al. "Counting Inconsistencies: An Analysis of American Jewish Population Studies with a Focus on Jews of Color," Berman Jewish

DataBank, 2019, https://www.jewishdatabank. org/content/upload/bjdb/2019_Counting_ Inconsistencies_Methodological_Appendix_Focus_ on_Jews_of_Color.pdf; accessed 15 July 2022

14. McKinney-Baldon, Shahanna. "I helped coin the term 'Jews of color.' It's time for a history lesson," *Jewish News*, July 2020, https://washtenawjewishnews.org/ PDFs/WJN-07-20-web.pdf; accessed 14 July 2022, p. 10

15. Sales, Ben. "In antisemitic rant, podcaster calls guest Jewish American Princess," *Jerusalem Post*, 13 July 2021, https://www.jpost.com/diaspora/antisemitism/ fashion-podcaster-accused-of-antisemitism-for-anti- racism-podcast-673667; accessed 14 July 2022

16. Kagan, Jack. "The Nazi arrived and started a selection," British Library, https://www.bl.uk/ learning/histcitizen/voices/testimonies/ghettos/ nazisarrive/selection.html; accessed 14 July 2022

ACKNOWLEDGMENTS

I want to thank my third-grade teacher who said Mizrahim have no culture. This one's for you.

To my mother Cami, my father Yakov, and brother Ben, thank you for being such an important part of my life and for loving me unconditionally.

Thanks to my partner, Marc, for admiring my story and always encouraging me to keep moving forward. You are my rock.

To Dr. Ron Katz, the president of the Tel Aviv Institute, I am grateful for the guidance and support that I have received—and no less for the encouragement and love I received from Rena Katz.

To David Hazony, whose experience was invaluable in the process of writing this book, thank you. Thanks to Max Rosenblum, who worked with me for hours to bring order to the ideas and experiences which are the underpinning of this story. I owe you a debt of gratitude.

To my friend whom I adopted as my sister, Ada Danelo, her partner Cara and her daughter Lucia, whose love and support have been a shining light at the end of every tunnel, thank you.

To my remarkable aunts, uncles, and cousins, wonderfully too many to name, thank you all. Itzik and Henriette, her father Sven, and their daughters Dana and Maian have been like second parents and sisters to me throughout my whole life. My world would be a far less remarkable place without the benefit of their wisdom. To my dear friends Sagy Cohen, Regev Yehezkel, Dean Leibovitz and Ofek Stern who have always been there for me. And to my friends and supporters Keren Hajioff, Tamara Towbin and Sarah Gipoor, thank you for your love.

And finally, I cannot say enough to my many dear friends in Israel and abroad whose presence in my heart and mind have added immeasurable richness to my life and work.

I wish Mark Bloom (z"l) were here to see this. He believed in me, saw the potential in me that I had yet to discover in myself, and took me under his wing. In these pages I honor you and your legacy. May your soul be bound up in the bond of everlasting life.

If there was ever a woman of strength and character, it is my grandmother Hela. Despite impossible odds, she not only survived but thrived. I love you, and I hope this book will be some recompense for what you have endured.

ABOUT THE AUTHOR

For a decade, Hen Mazzig has been an educator on Jews of the Middle East and North Africa, and credited by several historians as the founder of Mizrahi Heritage Month. Mazzig has appeared as an expert on Jewish issues on four continents, over five hundred college campuses, BBC, Sky News, TEDx, and countless Shabbat dinners.

Mazzig's writings have appeared in the *Los Angeles Times*, *Newsweek*, *NBC News*, *Haaretz*, *the Forward*, *Jewish Chronicle*, *International Business Times*, and numerous other publications. For his work inspiring thousands worldwide with his story, he was named in *Algemeiner*'s "Top 100 People Positively Influencing Jewish Life" in 2018 and 2021, the top fifty online pro-Israel influencers, and top fifty LGBTQ+ influencers.

Mazzig is a prominent digital influencer; over one hundred million users have interacted with his content, while his Instagram account has a higher engagement rate than those of Kim Kardashian, Cristiano Ronaldo, and Nike. He has authored numerous viral campaigns such as #JewishPrivilege, where he inspired others to speak out about the falsehood of Jews having advantages in modern society, and #JewishLooking, where thousands of Jews celebrated the ethnic and racial diversity of the community.

In 2019, Mazzig co-founded the Tel Aviv Institute, a non-profit dedicated to using data-driven social media strategies to stand up for Jewish people and other minorities online. As the Institute's senior fellow, he has trained a dynamic roster of Jewish advocates in messaging and has empowered a new generation of Jews to use publications, Twitter, Facebook, TikTok, and new media to advocate for tolerance and peace.

Mazzig grew up in Israel as the son of Mizrahi Jewish refugees from Iraq and Tunisia. He is a descendant of the indigenous tribe of North Africa, the Amazigh. As a young Israeli, Hen served in the Israel Defense Forces for almost five years as an openly gay commander. As a lieutenant in the Coordinator of Government Activities in the Territories unit, he was a humanitarian officer. While serving in the West Bank, Mazzig was an intermediary between the IDF, the Palestinian Authority, the UN, and many non-governmental organizations. He oversaw the construction of medical facilities, schools, environmental projects, roads, water-related infrastructure, and security coordination with the Palestinian Security Forces, part of the Palestinian Authority. A staunch advocate for the queer community, he served as the head of the Transgender and Health Department at Israel's National LGBTQ Task Force (the Nir Katz Center) in Tel Aviv.

Mazzig holds a BA in Middle Eastern and Jewish studies from Bar-Ilan University.

info@henmazzig.com

Made in United States
North Haven, CT
23 October 2022

25822708R00146